CLB 1381
Produced for Steimatzky Ltd., by Colour Library Books Ltd.
Copyright © 1985 Illustrations: Colour Library Books Ltd., Guildford, Surrey, England.
Copyright © 1985 Text: Steimatzky Ltd., P O B 628 Tel Aviv, Israel.
Printed and bound in Barcelona, Spain.
All rights reserved.
ISBN 0.86283.390.6

COLORFUL
ISRAEL

Text by
YADIN ROMAN

STEIMATZKY LTD.

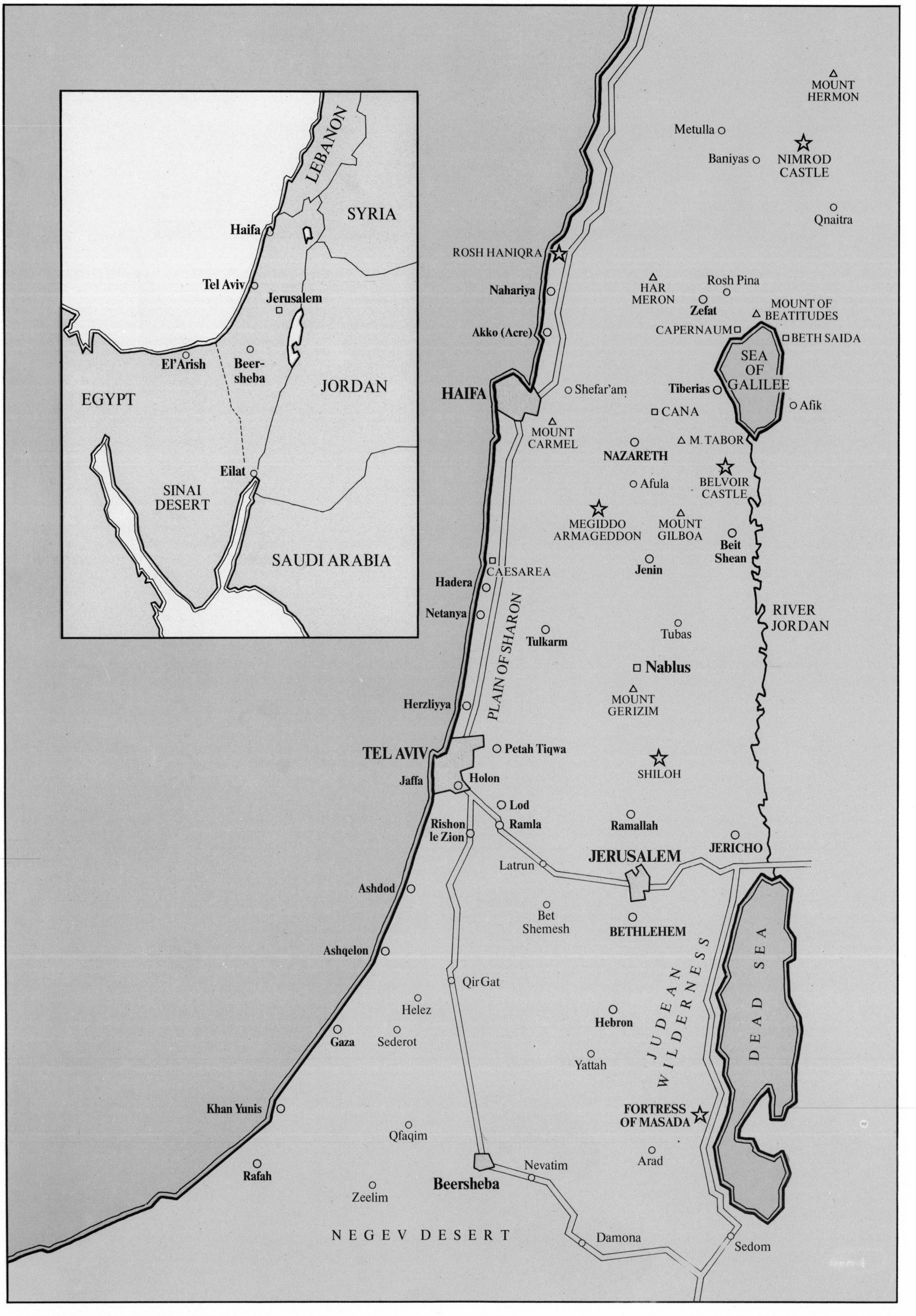
LEBANON
SYRIA
Haifa
Tel Aviv
Jerusalem
El'Arish
Beer-
sheba
JORDAN
EGYPT
Eilat
SINAI
DESERT
SAUDI ARABIA
MOUNT
HERMON
Metulla
Baniyas
NIMROD
CASTLE
Qnaitra
ROSH HANIQRA
Nahariya
HAR
MERON
Rosh Pina
Zefat
MOUNT OF
BEATITUDES
CAPERNAUM
BETH SAIDA
Akko (Acre)
SEA
OF
GALILEE
HAIFA
Shefar'am
Tiberias
Afik
CANA
MOUNT
CARMEL
M. TABOR
NAZARETH
BELVOIR
CASTLE
Afula
MEGIDDO
ARMAGEDDON
MOUNT
GILBOA
Beit
Shean
CAESAREA
Jenin
Hadera
Netanya
PLAIN OF SHARON
RIVER
JORDAN
Tulkarm
Tubas
Nablus
MOUNT
GERIZIM
Herzliyya
TEL AVIV
Petah Tiqwa
SHILOH
Jaffa
Holon
Lod
Rishon
le Zion
Ramla
Ramallah
JERICHO
JERUSALEM
Latrun
Ashdod
Bet
Shemesh
BETHLEHEM
Ashqelon
JUDEAN
WILDERNESS
DEAD SEA
Qir Gat
Helez
Hebron
Gaza
Sederot
Yattah
Khan Yunis
FORTRESS
OF MASADA
Qfaqim
Arad
Rafah
Beersheba
Nevatim
Zeelim
NEGEV DESERT
Damona
Sedom

Many lands offer vistas that are far more colossal than those of Israel. Few countries, though, have been so ornately chiseled by the hand of history – or have made as strong a mark on it.

Man already settled here in organized communities thousands of years ago. The oldest city in the world, Jericho, has existed for nine thousand years.

The father of monotheism, Abraham, was led here by the one God. "Go from your country and your kindred to the land that I will show you," he was commanded (Gen. 12:1), and he obeyed. His son and grandson, Isaac and Jacob, walked the width and length of the land. Moses, the lawgiver, led the people of Israel out of Egypt back to the land, though he was never to enter it himself.

Kings and prophets who have shaped the Western world's concepts of justice and righteousness lived and created here. Christianity was born here and some of the most sacred events in Islam's history took place here. Greeks, Romans, Byzantines, Persians, Moslems, Crusaders, Mamelukes, Turks, and British, have all ruled the land.

And in the past 100 years, the Jews have striven for the rebirth of their state here.

Israel is an irresistible beacon, summoning the traveler to journey through time among its ancient towns, holy sites, archaeological treasures, diverse traditions, and the people and places that are today, in their turn, intensely caught up in world events.

In these pages we have attempted to preserve in words and pictures the essence of a land that has captured the imagination of millions of people over thousands of years.

We hope it will help keep Israel with you until your next visit.

Jerusalem

It has been said that "ten measures of beauty descended on the world; nine were taken by Jerusalem." But where does that beauty lie?

I have often asked myself what it is that draws people to Jerusalem. Why does the very mention of the name "Jerusalem" stir up so much emotion, even among those who have never set eyes on the city? What is it about Jerusalem that lingers in the minds of people all over the world and has inspired artists and writers to devote so much creative energy to envisioning it without even having visited there?

As I walk about modern, everyday Jerusalem I wonder again about its beauty and fascination. Major parts of it are downright ugly. Jaffa Road, its main shopping street, is lined with dingy buildings and polluted by the exhaust fumes and clamor of dense vehicular traffic. Its quaint old quarters are a jumble of unkempt structures, overloaded with makeshift additions. Most of its new dwellings look like matchboxes attached to stone facings and topped with TV antennas.

The city's beauty transcends these mundane aspects. It radiates from Jerusalem's timeless, "celestial" features: the rugged hills, the gentle valleys, the ancient olive trees, and, most of all, the momentous events it has witnessed.

Viewed objectively, the Western Wall, for example, is just a wall – not very large and not particularly interesting. It is, however, a site of paramount importance for the hundreds of thousands of visitors who throng Jerusalem each year. For it is not what we see, neither the stones nor the plaza in front of it, but the history built into that wall, the fact that it was part of the wall that surrounded the Second Temple, that gives it meaning: "stones with a human heart," as a popular Israeli song goes.

Actually, most of the events in Jerusalem's history were of very little significance to those who did not live here. How many visitors are impressed that Jerusalem was ruled by the Mamelukes, or have heard of the Crusader ruler Baldwin II, the Ottoman leader Bayzid I, or Modestus, the bishop who built so much of the city? How many can tell of the accomplishments of the British governor Sir Ronald Storrs?

The world cherishes Jerusalem because its history is intertwined with the history of the three great monotheistic faiths. Jerusalem was the city where David and Solomon forged the Jewish nation, the city from which the great prophets issued the universal messages of social justice and righteousness that are the cornerstones of Judaism, the city in which a temple was built for the worship of the one God.

From the mountain on which this temple stood, another message was sent forth: the message of brotherly love preached by Jesus Christ. The Judeo-Christian heritage influenced the shaping of yet another great faith, Islam. The Moslems, in their belief that Mohammed ascended to heaven from the Temple Mount, have made Jerusalem one of their holy cities, second only to Mecca and Medina.

The visitors flocking to Jerusalem's holy sites, museums, and other landmarks want to see, breathe the air of, be a part of, the birthplace of the ideas which have so deeply affected their lives and the lives of their forebears. They want to walk where the heroes and prophets of the Old Testament, New Testament, and Koran walked, and experience for themselves the roots of their faith.

Let us, therefore, take a look at Jerusalem as the environment that nurtured these faiths.

The City of David

Sometimes it seems as if King David is right at your side, sitting in the next car at the traffic light, driving home from an afternoon on the rooftops of the city. For Jerusalem belongs to him.

True, its Gihon spring and fortress-like locale attracted dwellers long before David appeared on the scene. We can find evidence of its growth in the El Amarna tablets, which comprise the archives kept by the Egyptian foreign ministry 3,500 years ago – four hundred years before David came to Jerusalem. Those tablets show that Jerusalem was already populated enough for its ruler, King Abdi Khipa, to write six letters to the Pharaoh of Egypt, pleading for help because it was exploding with uprisings.

It was David, however, who was to be the deciding factor in the fate of the city.

When David was thirty years old, the leaders of the tribes of Israel came to him in Hebron and asked him to rule over them. Thus began David's forty-year reign which lasted until his death.

For the first seven years he ruled the Israelites from Hebron, the capital city of the tribe of Judah and the southern tribes. But he was not just another ruler of the tribal confederation of the people of Israel. He planned to forge the tribes into one nation, and for that purpose he needed a capital – not a regional, tribal capital like Hebron, but a national capital, conquered and built by the whole nation.

His eyes fell on Jerusalem, not far from his birthplace, Bethlehem. It was near the territory of the tribe of Benjamin, the tribe to which Saul, the former king of Israel, belonged, a tribe not clearly affiliated with any part of the tribal confederation. Jerusalem was still held by the Jebusites, the former inhabitants of the Land of Israel.

David carried out a surprise maneuver: his forces entered the city through its underground water system. Jerusalem was overpowered "And David dwelt in the stronghold and called it the city of David." (II Samuel, 5:9)

He did not have much time to consolidate his victory. The Philistines, the arch-enemies of the Israelites, perceived his motives and understood that a strong, united Israel was not in their interests. They invaded David's territory in full force, and for the next few years David was engaged in warding off the Philistines, ultimately routing them.

During that time he also unified the people of Israel, building up a central administration, central leadership, and central capital. Once the battlefields were quiet, David began to carry out the next step of his grand design: to make Jerusalem not only the capital of his kingdom but a religious center as well. Toward that end, the Ark of the Covenant, containing the tablets of the Ten Commandments, was brought to Jerusalem. It had been kept in a little village to the west of the city since its return from the hands of the Philistines, who had captured it from the Israelites in battle a few years before.

David led the procession "leaping and dancing before the Lord" (II Samuel 6:16), and slowly they advanced along a route which was probably similar to that of today's Tel Aviv-Jerusalem highway. The Ark was brought into the city of David and placed in a tent.

Previous pages: a moment of solitude at the
Western Wall. Facing page: the Citadel.

David wanted to build a temple for God in Jerusalem, but God came to the prophet Nathan in a vision and instructed him to tell David that the temple would be built only by the next king.

There may also have been a strong national resistance to the building of a temple. The nation was too young, the people were still tribesmen, a nomadic existence was still an ideal, and permanent dwellings were still looked upon with disdain. It was premature to build a permanent house for the God of the people of Israel.

David waited until the last years of his reign to broach again the subject of building a temple.

The last chapter of II Samuel describes this endeavor in detail. David was now in his late sixties, a very old age for that period, especially for a man who had spent most of his life fighting. A terrible plague had just struck the Israelites and they regarded it as God's way of expressing wrath against David's census of the population.

The Angel of God stood on a threshing floor which belonged to Arau'nah the Jebusite, on a mountain above the city of David. On seeing the angel, David asked for forgiveness, and the reply came through Gad, the prophet Nathan's successor in Jerusalem: "Go up, rear an altar to the Lord on the threshing floor of Arau'nah the Jebusite." (II Samuel 24:18)

Previous pages: Jews from all over the world come to Jerusalem to pray at the Western Wall. Women, who are not permitted in the men's section, view a bar mitzvah ceremony from their side of the divider. Facing page: Zecharia's

Tomb and other Second Temple period tombs in the Kidron Valley at the foot of the Mount of Olives. Above: ancient tombstones on the slopes of the Mount of Olives.

David climbed up the mountain to the place where the angel had stood. Arau'nah, seeing David and his courtiers ascending, rushed out to greet them. He bowed down before David, asking, "Why has my lord the king come to his servant?" David replied, "To buy the threshing floor of you, in order to build an altar to God, that the plague may be averted from the people."

"Let my lord the king take and offer up what seems good to him; here are the oxen for the burnt offering, and the threshing sledges and the yokes of the oxen for the wood. All this, O king, Arau'nah gives to the king." David answered, "No, but I will buy it of you for a price; I will not offer burnt offerings to the Lord my God which cost me nothing." (II Samuel 24:21-24)

He bought the threshing floor and the oxen for fifty silver shekels, "And David built there an altar to the Lord." (II Samuel, 24:25)

The stage had now been set for the building of a house of God in Jerusalem. David's brilliant son, Solomon, would carry out that task.

By the end of David's reign Jerusalem had become a big city. The kingdom had been expanded enormously by David and his army, and from Jerusalem Solomon ruled over the nation of Israel, the Edomites, the Aramites, the Ammonites, the Philistines, the people of Geshur and Maacha in the north, and many more. Visitors from all over the kingdom streamed into Jerusalem to attend to the business of the state in its capital city. The time had come to create the jewel in the capital's crown, the Temple of the Lord.

Solomon formed an alliance with Hiram, the king of Tyre (in today's Lebanon) and that country's architects were among the master builders of the Temple; cedars and cypresses were brought from Lebanon for timber.

A complex of buildings was constructed on Mount Moriah, including the Temple itself, which stood in the holy inner courtyard of the Temple Mount: a monumental Hall of Pillars, which served as the entrance to the whole complex; the Hall of the Throne, which was the seat of judgment; the House of the Forest of Lebanon, which was probably a storage area; the House of the King; and a house for the Pharaoh's daughter, Solomon's principal wife.

Since the eighteenth century, scholars and scientists have tried to envision the Temple. There are many descriptions of it in the Bible, but most of them do not facilitate reconstruction and contain many contradictory details.

What is certain is that it was an immense stone building. The walls were covered with cedar and the floors with cypress. The wood was carved with interconnecting reliefs, with a floral design. The wood paneling on the floors, the doors, and probably the ceiling was coated with gold. The perimeter was lined with a series of thirty-three connected cells. The main part of the Temple was divided into three sections. The innermost section was the Holy of Holies, which contained the Ark of the Covenant beneath two gold angels.

In the hall of the Temple, the room immediately preceding the Holy of Holies, stood a gold altar and a gold table or, according to the Book of Chronicles, ten gold tables — five along the left wall and five along the right wall. The hall also contained gold candelabra — five on the left and five on the right — with gold candles in them.

Facing page: For many people, a visit to the
Western Wall is a highly emotional experience.

Left and facing page, left: a model of Jerusalem at the time of the Second Temple, exhibited in the grounds of the Hoyland Hotel, provides a useful and interesting introduction to the city. Above: the Western Wall. Facing page, right: the Citadel, once the fortress guarding the palace of Herod the Great.

A large stone altar stood in the holy courtyard in front of the Temple, along with two large pillars which were called "Yachin" and "Boaz"; a large, copper water receptacle about 15 feet in diameter which held over 8,000 gallons of water, supported by twelve copper oxen; and ten bronze basins for ceremonial ablutions, on ornate copper stands.

In front of the Temple Solomon also placed the copper serpent, which was fashioned according to Moses' orders during the wanderings of the Israelites in the desert.

When the Temple was completed and Solomon had placed the Holy Ark in it, "a cloud filled the house of the Lord... for the glory of the Lord filled the house of the Lord." (I Kings 8:10)

King Solomon "stood before the altar of the Lord, in the presence of all the assembly of Israel... and said:... But will God indeed dwell on the earth? Behold, heaven and the highest heaven cannot contain thee; how much less this house which I have built!" (I Kings 8:22-27).

He beseeched God "That thy eyes may be open night and day toward this house, the place of which thou has said, 'My name shall be there,' that thou mayest hearken to the prayer which thy servant offers toward this place." (I Kings 8:29)

Solomon requested:
"Likewise when a foreigner, who is not of thy people Israel, comes from a far country

for thy name's sake..., when he comes and prays toward this house, hear thou in heaven thy dwelling place, and do according to all for which the foreigner calls to thee; in order that all the peoples of the earth may know thy name and fear thee, as do thy people Israel, and that they may know that this house which I have built is called by thy name." (I Kings 8:41-43)

Jerusalem thereby became a place of prayer, supplication, and forgiveness for the people of Israel and for the stranger, too – a universal city with a universal God.

The unity of David and Solomon's kingdom was not to last. With the death of Solomon it divided into two kingdoms, Israel and Judah. The northern kingdom, Israel, was the more powerful. Its capital moved with the various dynasties from Shechem to Tirza to Jezreel to Shomron, which gave the region the name Samaria. Its downfall came in 721 BC at the hands of the Assyrians. The inhabitants were exiled, the exiles

assimilated, and the people of the kingdom of Israel disappeared. The southern kingdom of Judah came to an end in 587 BC when Jerusalem was sacked and the Temple destroyed. But David, the redheaded soldier-king, and Solomon, his brilliant son, had created in Jerusalem a concept which was to endure for millennia. Jerusalem was to remain the center of the Jewish nation and people.

What was created nearly 3,000 years ago has withstood the battering of time.

There was, nevertheless, some weakening in allegiance to Jerusalem and its Temple after the division of the kingdom.

Even before Solomon died, outside influences had begun to permeate Israel. Solomon himself married foreign women, and in his old age "his wives turned his heart after other gods; and his heart was not wholly true to the Lord his God..." (I Kings 11:4) In fact, according to I Kings 11:9-39, it was precisely because of Solomon's defection from monotheism that God perpetrated the strife in the kingdom after his death.

Solomon's successors constructed alternatives to the Temple in the ancient places of worship. Golden calves were erected in Bethel and Dan and altars to foreign gods were built in Shechem, Shiloh, Mount Carmel, atop other high mountains, and under ancient trees.

Nonetheless, the symbol of the Jewish religion, the Ark of the Covenant between the people and the one God, remained in Jerusalem.

Warfare and Prophetic Warnings

New world powers were emerging. The Egyptians were consolidating in the southwest and for a time their influence would be felt again in Israel and Syria.

The most important global development, however, came from the northeast. First, the Syrian kingdoms broke away from Israel's rule and formed their own city-states. In the ninth century BC one of these units, the Syrian state of Aram-Damascus, grew stronger and more menacing, and persistently fought with Israel and Judah, generally triumphing.

In the middle of the ninth century BC, an even greater threat, the Assyrians, stormed out of the east into Israel and Judah and commenced a reign of terror. The fate of the people of Israel and Judah was now in the hands of people who worshipped other gods and it seemed as if these gods were much more powerful than the God of Israel. The Israelites could not understand how such a situation was possible: why couldn't the omnipotent God respond to their supplications at the Holy Temple?

At this point a new message was to come out of Jerusalem. Those who spread it were a new breed of people, the prophets, who received the word of God in dreams and visions. The warnings, admonitions, and reassurances they uttered ring as clearly today as they did when they were first spoken.

Amos, Micah, Haggai, Isaiah, Ezekiel and Jeremiah were among those whose prophecies conveyed a new interpretation of the world and its events.

What they told their kings and fellow Jews was that the Arameans, the Assyrians, and the Babylonians were actually messengers of the one God, serving as instruments for the punishment of the people of Israel and Judah, who had turned away from God, allowed injustice to prevail, robbed the poor, and become corrupt.

Jeremiah told the people of Jerusalem, "Then the Lord said unto me, out of the north evil shall break forth upon all the inhabitants of the land. For, lo, I am calling all the tribes of the kingdoms of the north, says the Lord; and they shall come and every one shall set his throne at the entrance of the gates of Jerusalem... And I will utter my judgments against them, for all their wickedness in forsaking me..." (Jeremiah 1:14-16)

"Your princes are rebels and companions of thieves," said Isaiah. "Every one loves a bribe and runs after gifts. They do not defend the fatherless, and the widow's cause does not come to them... I will restore your judges as at the first, and your counsellors as at the beginning. Afterward you shall be called the city of righteousness, the faithful city. Zion shall be redeemed by justice..." (Isaiah 1:23-27)

It was no simple matter to say such things in Jerusalem. At first, when the city was undergoing an economic boom, these prophecies were ridiculed. As the situation changed, however, and God's messengers of wrath threatened the city, the reaction to the prophecies turned to fear and hostility.

The prophets were brave, lonely men. Jeremiah's family hounded him, the townspeople threatened his life, and in his despair he cried out to God, "But, O Lord of

Facing page: detail from the sixteenth-century city walls. Overleaf: the Dome of the Rock, one of Islam's most holy shrines.

Hosts, who judgest righteously, who triest the heart and the mind, let me see thy vengeance upon them, for to thee have I committed my cause." (Jeremiah, 11:20)

Amos was told to leave Bethel, where he had gone to preach. Amos, a herdsman from Tekoah, to the south of Jerusalem, gave the retort: "Now therefore hear the word of the Lord. You say, 'Do not prophesy against Israel, and do not preach against the house of Isaac.' Therefore thus says the Lord: 'Your wife shall be a prostitute in the city, and your sons and your daughters shall fall by the sword...'" (Amos 7:16-17)

The prophets also envisioned salvation, but only if the people would repent: "Comfort, comfort my people, says your God," says Isaiah. "Speak tenderly to Jerusalem, and cry to her that her warfare is ended, that her iniquity is pardoned, that she has received from the Lord's hand double for all her sins." (Isaiah 40:1-2)

Jerusalem was destroyed by the Babylonians in 587 BC, and the people of Judah were exiled to Babylon. The siege of the city and the exile were witnessed by Jeremiah. He was already a very old man and he had lived to see his prophecies come true. Throughout the battle he preached against resistance to God's will; he spent most of that period in prison.

The desolation of the city was described in the Book of Lamentations, which some scholars contend was also written by Jeremiah. "All who pass along the way clap their hands at you; they hiss and wag their heads at the daughter of Jerusalem; 'Is this the city which was called the perfection of beauty, the joy of all the earth?'" (Lamentations 2:15)

The king of Babylon, who had heard of Jeremiah, wanted to offer him favored treatment. He eventually found him plodding along beside his fellow exiles on the way to Babylon. Jeremiah rejected the king's offer, but decided to go back to Judah and stay there with the remaining Jews.

Those who stayed behind rose up against the Babylonian conquerors a few years later, and subsequently fled to Egypt. Jeremiah was among them, and died alone in an obscure Egyptian town, far away from his beloved Jerusalem.

The Israelites in Babylon yearned for Jerusalem: "By the waters of Babylon, there we sat down and wept, when we remembered Zion... How shall we sing the Lord's song in a foreign land?" They vowed, "If I forget you, O Jerusalem, let my right hand wither! Let my tongue cleave to the roof of my mouth, if I do not remember you, if I do not set Jerusalem above my highest joy!" (Psalms 137:1-6)

They looked to Isaiah's prophecy for comfort: "...your ancient ruins shall be rebuilt; you shall raise up the foundations of many generations..." (Isaiah 58:12)

For fifty years Jerusalem lay neglected.

In 539 BC, Cyrus, king of Persia, conquered Babylon. The Persians had an enlightened attitude toward conquest – and a need for a friendly, grateful nation on their southern border. Accordingly, in 538 BC, Cyrus proclaimed that the exiles from Judah could re-turn to Jerusalem and rebuild the Temple there. (Ezra 1:2-4 and II Chronicles 36:22-23)

This proclamation was not greeted by a mass exodus; apparently, most of the exiles had settled comfortably into their new surroundings by then. Only 42,360 people made their way back to Jerusalem that year, led by Sheshbazzar, probably son of Yehoyachin, the exiled king of Judah. Another small contingent, led by Zerubabel, Yehoyachin's grandson, arrived two years later.

The returnees found that a new people had taken their place in Jerusalem: the Samaritans, foreign tribes brought into the city at the time of the exile. These immigrants had adopted Jewish traditions without officially converting, and intermarried with the local Jews who had not been taken to Babylon. They wanted to be part of the effort to rebuild the Temple, but were harshly rejected by Zerubabel, who refused to recognize them as fellow Jews.

The Samaritans ultimately moved the center of their activities to Mount Grizim, in Samaria. For the next eight years, however, their bitter opposition, the hostility of other inhabitants of the city, and the returnees' own foot-dragging held up the beginning of construction of the new Temple.

When the project was actually launched, Zerubabel enlisted all of the returned exiles to help in the work, and relied on the spiritual assistance of the prophets Haggai and Zecharia. But he was not to see the task completed: he mysteriously vanished from history a few years later, probably in the wake of the brutally suppressed Jewish uprising against the Persians in 518 BC.

Above left: the Church of Mary Magdalene, on the Mount of Olives. Above right and top right: crowds throng the Church of the Holy Sepulchre during the Greek Orthodox Ceremony of Holy Fire. Facing page: the entrance to the Church of the Holy Sepulchre.

The Temple was completed three years later, twenty-three years after Cyrus issued his proclamation. By this time the returnees to Judah had become a nation, headed by a high priest.

In 457 BC, Ezra, a scribe for the Persian court, arrived in Jerusalem from Babylon. In 445 BC, Nehemiah, another Jewish official from Babylon, was sent to Jerusalem as a representative of the king of Persia. These two men laid the foundations for the new Jerusalem and the new Jewish commonwealth.

Nehemiah ordered and supervised the construction of the walls of the city and many of its buildings. He secured a Jewish presence in the city, mainly by establishing an economic base and decreeing that every tenth Jewish family in the land (chosen by lot) had to move to Jerusalem. Ezra compiled the rulings and laws that gave Judaism the form we know today. The Jewish population of Jerusalem steadily grew.

In 332 BC, Alexander the Great of Macedonia overthrew the Persians and Hellenism arrived in the region, not bypassing Jerusalem. Alexander's successors ruled Jerusalem from Egypt (the Ptolemies) and from Antioch (the Seleucids). In the second century BC, Antiochus Epiphanes, the last great Seleucid king, tried to force Hellenism on all of his subjects. The Jews rebelled in 167 BC and, after Antiochus' death, a new, independent Jewish commonwealth was created under the Hasmoneans (Maccabees).

By the second half of the first century BC, when Herod was appointed king of Judah by the Romans, Jerusalem was one of the largest cities in the world. It was the home of 200,000 people and hosted an additional 500,000 visitors to the Temple annually, most of them streaming into the city, 100,000 strong, on the three occasions a year which required a pilgrimage to the Temple.

The 500-year-old Temple was ill-equipped to receive such tremendous crowds, nor could the narrow approaches to it cope with the heavy onslaught of two-way traffic. Herod decided to redesign the Temple and its environs, preparing a grand plan that would use sophisticated methods of "people-movement." It was the most tremendous building project ever to be executed in Jerusalem – and the city has never again witnessed one of such scope.

Many obstacles stood in Herod's way. The measurements of the Temple were sacred and could not be altered. Worship in the Temple could not be interrupted. The only people allowed into the innermost sections of the Temple were priests. The whole area around the Temple was very heavily populated. The main problem, though, was the Jewish leadership's distrust of Herod.

He nevertheless managed to obtain the support of the Jewish leaders and organized a major campaign for the purchase of land in which to resettle the inhabitants of the areas slated for redevelopment. Fifteen thousand people were trained as a work force, including one thousand priests.

Before work could actually begin on the existing structure, all of the stone to be used in rebuilding the Temple was quarried so that the disturbance to the prayers in the Temple would not be prolonged each time it was necessary to replenish the supply. For eight years, all of the components of the Temple were assembled around it.

Herod created a huge, 96-foot-high platform on which the Temple stood and the people could gather. Elaborate entrances and exits were built, with overpasses, underpasses, bridges, and stairways into and out of the Temple.

A modern road system was built around the Temple, with a main through-road along the exterior of the Temple's western wall. It was 39 feet wide, over a mile long, and had shops along both its sides. From this through-road stairways, bridges, and roads provided access to the Temple and the other parts of the city.

One of the bridges leading from the road to the southern part of the Temple was the largest arch ever constructed in the Roman world; it was suspended over 90 feet above the road, was 39 feet wide and weighed over 1,000 tons.

When the project was completed, Jerusalem became one of the most modern cities in the world.

To this bustling metropolis came Jesus and his disciples, after their journey around the Galilee. Jesus took one look at the newly designed Temple Mount and declared that the commercial activities were too close to the holy Temple. He vented his wrath on the merchants of Jerusalem.

In this great city, Jesus was marched through the streets carrying the cross to his own crucifixion. News of this event, witnessed by crowds of inhabitants and visitors to Jerusalem, spread rapidly.

The Temple survived for another 40 years, and then, after four years of bitter fighting between the Jewish rebels and the Romans, Jerusalem was destroyed once again, its Temple and its buildings set ablaze. In 70 AD, on the ninth of the month of Av, worship at the Temple ceased for the first time in 565 years. One month later the city of Jerusalem lay in ruins.

After the destruction of the Temple, the city became an encampment for the Tenth Roman Legion. The situation did not change until the futile Jewish attempt to regain independence, led by Bar Kochba, in 132-135 AD. Following Bar Kochba's defeat, Emperor Hadrian decided to create a pagan city in Jerusalem. He began rebuilding the city, which he renamed Aelia Capitolina in his own honor ("Aelia" was Hadrian's Greek name).

When Christianity became the official religion of the Roman Empire, Jerusalem's rehabilitation was accelerated. Churches were constructed on the sites where the important events of Christianity had occurred and pilgrims again flocked to the city, this time to its Christian holy places. Jerusalem again underwent alterations to enable it to accommodate many visitors; a major addition was a new main thoroughfare, the Cardo, created primarily for religious processions.

In 636 the Moslems conquered Jerusalem. The Christians were permitted to remain and to worship in their churches, but the Moslems focused their own attention on the Temple Mount.

They regarded the Temple Mount as the entrance to heaven, the rock in the center of the Mount as the rock from which Mohammed ascended to heaven, and the site of the present-day al-Aqsa Mosque as the furthest point Mohammed reached on his Night Journey. Jerusalem, as the city encompassing these sites, was considered the holiest city in the world, after Mecca and Medina.

To mark their holy places, the Moslems built the el-Aqsa Mosque around 660 and the Dome of the Rock in 691. Huge palaces were built on the Temple Mount, which was now called Haram el-Sherif (The Holy Area).

Jerusalem was again beautified. The Moslems built palaces and religious schools. Once more, pilgrims – Moslems this time – filled the city.

In 1099 the First Crusade hurled itself at the walls of Jerusalem. Though they met with resistance by the Jews and Moslems, these "messengers of salvation" were much better prepared for the battle than the local inhabitants and brutally defeated them, massacring many and taking others captive.

The Crusaders ruled Jerusalem for nearly one hundred years. During that period it was once again the capital of an independent country, this time the Crusaders' kingdom, called "The Kingdom of Jerusalem," "The Jerusalemite Kingdom," and "The Kingdom of David." They built churches and hospices all over the city.

In 1187 the Crusaders were ousted by the Egyptian Moslems; they were later replaced by the Mamelukes, other Moslems who had taken over in Egypt. The Moslems built schools, mosques, and other religious institutions in the Holy Area.

The Moslem capital was in Egypt, and Jerusalem became a place of exile for many of the officals who had fallen from favor or were considered too dangerous to keep in Egypt.

In 1516 the Turks, led by Suleiman the Magnificent, conquered Egypt and made Jerusalem part of the Ottoman Empire for the next 400 years. In 1537 work began on new walls around the city, ordered by Suleiman. These walls are still standing in present-day Jerusalem. He also initiated repairs to the city's water system and the construction of the Sultan's Pool, a reservoir on the foundations of an ancient pool.

The city did not regain its former glory; it had the status of a small, insignificant town in a remote corner of the Ottoman Empire. Jerusalem declined into squalor, ruled by a disgruntled Turkish official out to make the most money he could from a bad situation.

By the nineteenth century Jerusalem's population had fallen to below 30,000. Then inhabitants of the walled city comprised four major ethnic groups: Moslems, who lived around the entrances to the Dome of the Rock; Armenians, who lived in a quarter that was in itself walled in; Christians, around the area of the Holy Sepulchre; and Jews, on the hill overlooking the Western Wall.

These ethnic groups were in turn splintered into many small groups, each led by a religious figure who attempted to obtain separate recognition from the Turkish officials in Jerusalem.

The largest and most rapidly growing group was the Jews. For the previous 400 years, Jews had been trickling into the city to settle near the holy sites. Most of them came to Jerusalem primarily to pray, and lived from contributions sent by Jewish communities all over the world, for the upkeep of those immigrants from their city or region.

Large Christian pilgrimages also arrived in the city during the Turkish period, most of them from Russia, Greece, Cyprus, and the Balkans. These groups were by their very nature only temporary residents, sojourning in the city for only three or four months. The Russian Orthodox Church looked after these pilgrims by building sizable hostels for them around the country, mainly in Jerusalem.

The Jews, however, came to stay, and the steady increase in their ranks resulted in a housing shortage in the already poorly equipped city. Jerusalem had no water system except cisterns which collected rainwater in the winter and a small spring from which

Previous pages and facing page: the Dome of the Rock; according to Moslem tradition, Mohammed ascended to heaven from the rock shown in the foreground.

water had to be hauled to the houses. Its sewer system dated back to the time of Herod the Great, its streets were dark and unpaved, the houses had no foundations and often collapsed, and walls tended to become damp from the water cisterns which were underneath the buildings.

Disease was rampant and was a main cause for comment and concern among those who visited the city. Karl Marx stated unequivocally, "I would not like to live in Jerusalem!" and Mark Twain satirized the generally neglected condition of the Holy City.

Most Jewish families lived in one-room apartments; sometimes even extended families lived together in these cramped quarters, with the newlyweds sharing a little, curtained-off alcove.

By the middle of the nineteenth century conditions were intolerable, and groups of Jews began to form organizations with the aim of doing the unthinkable: moving outside the city walls. This idea was thought of as preposterous by most Jews in the city. Outside the walls it was dangerous, there was no official protection, and most Jerusalemites believed that wild animals and ghosts inhabited the area at night. For some, however, moving outside the Old City walls was the only solution.

In the midst of this controversy arrived Sir Moses Montefiore, a wealthy English Jew, whose involvement with Jerusalem created the funds and environment which made resettlement possible. In 1857, he launched the development program by purchasing a large tract of land on the road to Hebron and erecting a hospital on it. This enterprise failed, as the sick were too frightened to sleep there.

Montefiore converted the hospital building to an agricultural enterprise which was meant to create jobs and income for the disadvantaged Jerusalemites. The centerpiece was a windmill which was intended to serve as a wheat mill for the region. All of the machinery and metal parts were painstakingly imported from England. When everything was assembled in Jerusalem, the engineering experts – who were also imported from England – discovered that there was not enough wind to turn the sails. The project failed.

Finally, in 1860, Montefiore's venture became a housing project. Very few people agreed to live in it in the beginning, but the precedent had been set: housing projects could be built outside the city walls. The next serious attempt at resettlement came seven years later, initiated by a group of seven Jewish families. This endeavor succeeded, and from then on more and more Jews moved into the western section of Jerusalem. A whole new Jewish city developed, and by World War I, a half-century later, over thirty new housing projects had been built there. A number of Arab building projects were being erected to the north of the Old City.

The pioneering work of Sir Moses Montefiore was not forgotten: many of the first neighborhoods built outside the Old City walls, as well as more recently established sections, are named after him and his family.

The Turkish Empire began to erode and the European powers became more influential in Jerusalem. Their representatives supervised the construction of churches, schools, hospitals, hospices, and other institutions all around the city.

With the onset of World War I, most of the diplomats left Jerusalem, and in December 1917 the Turks began to leave as well. On December 9, 1917, two privates from a British

Facing page: the Church of All Nations at Gethsemane.

Army encampment near Jerusalem went into the surrounding hills to look for water. To their surprise, they were met by an official delegation from Jerusalem, who offered them the surrender of the city. Hastily accepting, the two soldiers hurried back to their camp in order to arrange a more appropriate reception for the keys of the city.

The British, who had taken the whole of Palestine from the Turks, related to Jerusalem as a capital city, setting up administrative institutions there. They introduced urban planning, preparing a master plan for the entire city. In 1922 they passed an ordinance that all buildings in Jerusalem were to be constructed of Jerusalem stone. That ordinance is still in effect today; the only exceptions are some building in the outlying district and buildings constructed in the 1930s and '40s, when stone was extremely expensive and concrete was used instead. Attractive private and public buildings were erected and the city developed rapidly.

Just outside the Damascus Gate is the Garden Tomb (above left). Remaining pictures: on Good Friday crowds of pilgrims and sightseers proceed along the Way of the Cross, following Jesus' footsteps through the Old City of Jerusalem.

A storm was brewing, however. Though the British had received a mandate in 1920 from the League of Nations to establish a national home for the Jewish people in Palestine, Arabs, Jews, and the British were soon fighting over the fate of the country. On November 2, 1947, the United Nations decided to terminate the mandate and partition Palestine. The British left Palestine in 1948, the State of Israel was declared, and a full-scale war broke out between the Jews and Arabs. Seven armies of the surrounding Arab countries invaded Israel to prevent the establishment of Jewish and Palestinian states.

The Arabs living in Jerusalem and in the villages around it lay siege to the Jewish part of the city, which fought for its life with very little food and water. Jewish convoys, organized in the coastal area, pushed through to Jerusalem, fighting their way up the road from Tel Aviv. The newly born Israel Defense Forces built an alternative road to the city and managed to prevent the collapse of Jerusalem.

The Jordanian Arab Legion crossed the Jordan River and occupied the area to the west of the river. In the Old City of Jerusalem, bitter fighting broke out between the

Jews living in the Jewish Quarter and the Arabs surrounding it. The Arab Legion invaded the Old City and its troops joined the fierce hand-to-hand and house-to-house warfare in the city. The Jewish Quarter's inhabitants and defenders eventually surrendered and were taken prisoner by the Jordanians; they were released a year later.

By the end of the war, the city was divided between Jordan and the new state of Israel. The Arabs living in the Israeli sector (West Jerusalem) fled to the Jordanian sector (East Jerusalem), which included the Old City. A hostile border, laced with barbed wire, mines, and machine-gun positions, cut through the city.

The Jordanians had agreed to allow Jews to visit the Western Wall and to study at the Hebrew University on Mount Scopus, which was surrounded by the Arab Legion. However, the Wall remained just a far-off dream for the city's Jewish inhabitants and the only Israelis permitted entry to the university facilities on Mount Scopus were guards, changed every two weeks under the protection of the United Nations.

The sole meeting point between the two parts of the city was the Mandelbaum Gate, through which only UN officials and a few dignitaries and visiting VIPs could cross.

For the next 19 years Jewish Jerusalem, officially the capital of Israel, was a backwater town, hemmed in by hostile neighbors. The Jordanians built up their capital in Amman and treated East Jerusalem as just another city under their rule.

On June 5, 1967, the first day of the Six Day War, West Jerusalem was shelled by the Jordanians. Israel retaliated: its troops advanced on the Jordanian and Iraqi armies, and in three days Jerusalem was reunited.

Following its reunification, Jerusalem underwent dynamic development and expanded in area and population. In order to prevent the defacing of the city through hasty and reckless construction, an international advisory board, the Jerusalem Committee, was founded to create guidelines for city planning which would safeguard Jerusalem's historical and religious heritage.

As the centers of power and government moved to Jerusalem, many new jobs were created and the city's economy was given a big boost. The Hebrew University of Jerusalem redesigned its old campus on Mount Scopus which had been empty for nineteen years and the Scopus and Givat Ram campuses became intensively active centers of academic life.

Excavations were undertaken in the city to rediscover its ancient glory and each year dramatic finds are unearthed and opened to the public.

The Old City and its environs are being beautified: the walls have been cleared of 400 years of debris and stand again at their original height, surrounded by a "green belt" of attractive parks and archaeological gardens and crowned by a "Ramparts Walk" covering the perimeter of the Old City.

The streets of the Old City have been repaved, with many of their original Roman paving stones incorporated in the new pavements. Restoration work has been done on many landmarks and monuments, including the Church of the Holy Sepulchre, the Dome of the Rock, the el-Aqsa Mosque, the Western Wall, the Jewish Quarter, the Church of Saint Anne, the Church of the Redeemer, and many more.

The ancient Roman entrance of Jerusalem has been reopened, and the Ottoman Damascus Gate has been given a new approachway; the old dirt roads, covered in dust and mud, have been paved with stone, as in the days of Solomon and Herod. Modern telephone systems, electricity, sewers, and other utilities have been installed in the Old City, out of sight of the visitor.

Jerusalem has regained its status as a living, functioning capital. It is again a center for the forces which shape the present and future of the region. It is the focus of both Jewish and Palestinian aspirations.

Illuminated at night are the walls of Jerusalem, with the Jaffa Gate at the far left, the golden Dome of the Rock at the center, and the Mount of Olives rising beyond the city.

The present-day conflict between Jew and Arab, Israeli and Palestinian, is manifested very intensely in the microcosm of Jerusalem. The city thrives united and dies split apart. It is the tragedy, hope, and above all the symbol of the future of the whole area, even in the face of conflict, strife, and opposed interests.

Jerusalem's nearly 400,000 inhabitants live in a city that can boast 5,000 years of continued habitation – and look forward to the three-thousandth anniversary of King David's decision to make it the capital of the Jewish state.

Tel Aviv

On the 6th of July, 1906, a group of wealthy Jewish businessmen gathered at Jaffa's Yeshurun Club. Most of them had arrived in Palestine (then a province of the Ottoman Empire) a few years earlier, and opened businesses in Jaffa, which was the main port of the province.

Jaffa was a dilapidated little town but, during the last two decades of the nineteenth century and the first years of the twentieth, it had become the chief entrance port for the new wave of Jewish immigrants to Palestine.

Disembarking at Jaffa port was no easy matter. The ships anchored offshore and the passengers were transferred by launch to the ancient harbor from which Jonah set off to meet his whale.

New arrivals had to bribe the Turkish officials to admit them to the country. If the immigrant did not have money for a bribe he was in for an interminable wait until it was decided that he was indeed indigent and should be allowed entry "on the house."

Upon finally setting foot in town, the enthusiastic, romantic, idealistic pioneer was rudely awakened from his reverie by the sight of dirty streets, hordes of flies, and a welcoming committee of local hawkers eager to sell the poor greenhorn something before he caught on to the real prices of goods and to the fact that he might never receive the merchandise he had purchased.

The next shock for the immigrant was the discovery that housing was in horribly short supply and that he would have to stay at a hotel for a much longer period that he had expected.

Most of the Jewish immigrants arriving in those years were infused with a desire to settle and farm the land. They eventually found their way to one of the new Jewish pioneering farming communities which were springing up in Palestine, many of them not far from Jaffa.

Some did not want a farming life. Either they were not really meant for it and after a few years on the farms drifted back to Jaffa, or from the beginning they had decided to stay in the city, also choosing Jaffa. For most of the new arrivals, Jerusalem was too religious and lacked commercial opportunities. In addition, the traditional Jewish population living in Jerusalem frowned upon these new immigrants and their modern ideas of recreating a Jewish nation in its ancient homeland.

Life in Jaffa was extremely difficult, though, and at the end of the nineteenth century, Jaffa's Jews were already buying small parcels of land on the sand dunes to the north of the city and building themselves suburbs.

Jaffa was bordered on the east as far as the eye could see by groves of the famous Jaffa oranges, on the south by sand dunes and a large swamp, and on the north by lower sand dunes which stretched all the way from Jaffa to the Yarkon River, at that time still a real river whose waters flowed freely to the sea.

The group which had gathered that evening at the Yeshurun Club decided to found a new Jewish suburb outside the town limits of Jaffa. For that purpose, the group established a society which they called Ahuzat Bayit (housing estate) and elected a five-member committee to recruit participants in their venture.

The main difference between this group and the fourteen other groups which had already built themselves small suburbs around Jaffa, was that its members were all well-to-do business people who wanted their housing estate to be the very model of a modern, planned, Hebrew housing estate.

As nearly all of them had businesses in the town itself, they initially considered building the estate inside Jaffa proper, but eventually the dearth of available land in town forced the issue.

During the next two years the members of the committee persuaded more people to join, acquired loans from the new Jewish National Fund and the bank of the World Zionist Organization, the Anglo-Palestine Bank (later to become Bank Leumi), and bought a large tract of land in the dunes north of Jaffa.

On April 11, 1909, the sixty-six founders assembled on the sand dunes and lots were drawn for the first sixty plots in the new suburb. The land on which they stood is today part of Tel Aviv's business district.

Unlike the other new suburbs around Jaffa, this one had a master plan. The founders decided that, before building began, they would ask professional town planners to submit overall plans for the suburb.

The neighborhood would have spacious streets, the main street would be 36 feet wide, the side streets 30, and the streets would be paved and lit. A well would be dug and a pump with a reservoir installed on it. All the houses would have pipes connecting them to the reservoir. These features were striking innovations for the province of Palestine.

To give the suburb a uniformly flat topography, the land was meticulously levelled out.

Only when all the above improvements were completed were the plots allotted and construction launched. On May 30, 1909, the first house was built, and by November of that year fifty families were living there.

On May 21, 1909, the members of the Ahuzat Bayit Society decided to name their suburb Tel Aviv. Though the literal translation is "hill of spring," the name actually derives from *Altneuland* (Old-New Land), the title of the book written by Theodore Herzl, the father of modern Zionism. Tel, "ancient mount," symbolizes the fact that the land dates back to ancient times, and Aviv, "spring," symbolizes the renewal of the Jewish homeland.

Herzl's dream of rebuilding the Jewish national homeland impelled the builders of the new suburb. He had died at the young age of 44 only five years earlier, and the founders of Tel Aviv did not want his dream to die with him.

The main street of Tel Aviv, the street which began at the entrance to the suburb just across the Jaffa-Jerusalem railway tracks, was called Herzl Street. The nicest houses lined Herzl Street, and the other four streets intersected it.

At the other end of Herzl Street, on a sand dune overlooking the suburb, the crowning glory was built: the Herzliya Hebrew Gymnasium, the first Hebrew high school in Palestine. This modern Jewish high school had an all-Hebrew curriculum and many of its graduates became important public figures. Today, Tel Aviv's major skyscraper, the Shalom Tower, stands on the site of the Gymnasium.

The new suburb grew quickly. Many wanted to join, and additional plots of land were

acquired. Very soon, however, the initial careful planning of the suburb fell apart, for two main reasons. One was that the suburb grew too rapidly, and the new additions did not fit in with the town plan. The other was that the positioning of Herzliya Gymnasium – perpendicular to the end of Herzl Street to allow train passengers a full view of the school– had effectively sealed off Tel Aviv's official main thoroughfare from further development.

These problems were not yet apparent in those early years. The builders of Tel Aviv pushed through local ordinances which would preserve the atmosphere of the little garden suburb they had envisioned. The plans for each house had to be submitted for approval to the committee, no more than a third of the plot could be used for the actual building, and each house had to be at least three feet from the edge of the next plot. From the beginning, though, many of the ordinances were not obeyed, even by the founders and committee members. This disregard for town planning regulations is still prevalent in Tel Aviv today.

Special attention was devoted to landscaping. In 1911 one thousand trees were planted along Herzl Street. Rothschild Boulevard, which had become a major thoroughfare, was also landscaped, and all plot owners were required by law to plant trees on their property.

Soon, many large plots to the north and west of Tel Aviv were puchased by various groups. Though these tracts were not developed until World War I, they constituted a reserve for the subsequent rapid development of Tel Aviv.

By the outbreak of World War I in 1914, "Little Tel Aviv," as it was later nostalgically called, had mushroomed to 150 houses and nearly 2,000 inhabitants.

The British forces advanced on Palestine from the south and after a three-year stalemate at Gaza, they managed to break through the Turkish lines and begin their advance to northern Palestine.

On March 30, 1917, the eve of the Jewish festival of Passover, the Turkish commander of the front, Jemal Pasha, decided to deport all the Jews living in and around Jaffa. The area was going to be heavily fortified by the Turks, and he was afraid that if the British forces landed by sea, the Jewish population would by sympathetic to them.

The Jewish population of Jaffa and the surrounding suburbs, including Tel Aviv, was forced to leave, and in three days Tel Aviv and Jaffa were virtually bereft of Jews. Only a few were left to guard Tel Aviv.

In October, 1917, a Jewish, pro-British spy ring was discovered by the Turks when one of the ring's carrier pigeons landed in the headquarters of the Turkish military governor of Jaffa. This incident did not help matters for the deportees, who were scattered in the Jewish settlements in the north and center of the country. They endured hunger and disease, living in makeshift accommodation. Three hundred of them died during this period.

At the end of October, 1917, the British opened their attack on the south of the country, and in a month of fighting occupied the area between Beer Sheva and the Yarkon River to the north of Tel Aviv. The Yarkon River became a border between the British and the Turks.

With the British occupation of Tel Aviv the population began to return. The British crossed the Yarkon River in a surprise attack on the Turkish positions and by the autumn of 1918 Palestine was under British mandatory rule.

Previous pages and above: Jaffa, the largest metropolitan area in Israel – comprised of

Jaffa, the ancient port, and Tel Aviv; founded as a garden suburb of Jaffa in 1909.

British rule, with the Balfour Declaration stating that "His Majesty's Government looks with favor upon the establishment of a Jewish homeland in Palestine," and a new British civil administration headed by a Jewish high commissioner, Sir Herbert Samuel, created a spirit of euphoria among the Jewish settlers in Palestine.

The country was no longer a forgotten Turkish province to be covertly "infiltrated" by the Jewish immigrants: it was now a country officially designated as the homeland of the Jews.

Multitudes of new immigrants had to be brought into the country in order to build up the Jewish homeland, and money had to be invested in it for development. From now on the center of these national activities would be Tel Aviv, the little suburb outside Jaffa, which had been transformed into a modern, Jewish city.

In the first thirteen years of British rule, Tel Aviv grew from 2,000 inhabitants to 75,000 and the number of houses increased thirtyfold from 150 to 5,000. Its area grew to five times what it was at the beginning of World War I. Such stupendous growth in such a short time-span was extraordinary, not only for Israel, but for the world as well.

At the beginning of the 1920s two pivotal events in Tel Aviv's history occurred. The first involved a major step forward in the city's civic life. In 1921 the British decided to make Tel Aviv a separate township independent of Jaffa and, in 1922, the first Tel Aviv Town

Council was elected by a general assembly of the population, with Meir Dizengoff installed as the first mayor of the city.

The other event was a tragic one. On May 1-2, 1921, the Arabs of Jaffa, incited by extremists, rioted in Jaffa and on the outskirts of Tel Aviv, killing dozens of Jews. This violence spurred more Jews to move out of Jaffa and motivated expansion of Tel Aviv to the north, further away from Jaffa. As a result, Tel Aviv's status as a city in its own right was confirmed geographically.

Above: one of the broad streets of Tel Aviv-Jaffa which were filled with Israelis celebrating Independence Day 1980 (facing page).

In 1923 the new power plant built by Pinchas Rothenberg on the shores of the Mediterranean Sea, north of the Yarkon River, went into operation and Tel Aviv's streets and houses were linked to the electric grid.

Tel Aviv was no longer to be a quiet garden suburb meant only for residential purposes, where even the granting of a permit to install a refreshment stand aroused heated debate. (The stand was eventually approved and is still doing business today at its original site on Rothschild Boulevard.)

In 1921 a commercial center was built to the south of Tel Aviv's first houses. It was the first modern and planned commercial center in the country and was a focal point for most of the commercial activity of the Jews of Palestine.

Soon after the British authorities took power in Palestine they enacted town planning regulations and laws for the country. In 1925, the Scottish town planner Professor Patrick Geddes was invited to submit a general master plan for the city of Tel Aviv. He quickly discovered that the built-up areas of the city were impossible to plan or redesign, so he confined his plan to the northern section, which was not yet densely developed.

The plan set out the major roads and squares of the city, including Dizengoff Circle and the streets around it. Geddes placed several long, straight streets parallel to the seashore, with six streets intersecting them. This scheme has been the basis for the shape of Tel Aviv to this day, and the City Council continues to adhere as closely as possible to the guidelines set by Geddes.

By 1934, only twenty-five years after it was founded, Tel Aviv had become the largest city in Palestine, with 75% of the country's commerce, 37 banks, 65 hotels, 6 movie houses, and over 200 offices. That year it was granted municipal status.

Tel Aviv also became the national center of Hebrew culture. Many of Israel's modern poets, who revived Hebrew poetry and prose, lived in Tel Aviv. The most famous was Israel's national poet, Haim Nahman Bialik, who lived there for the last ten years of his life, 1924-1934. His house on today's Bialik Street, near the former site of the Municipality, was a meeting-place for artists and writers.

Bialik's house, the old Municipality building, and the house of one of Tel Aviv's prominent artists, Reuven Rubin, provide an insight into the Hebrew cultural revival of that period.

The national Hebrew theater, Habima (The Stage), founded in Moscow in 1918, now makes its home in Tel Aviv. The Habima building took ten years to complete and was officially opened in 1945.

The first concert ever given by the Israel Philharmonic Orchestra was presented at Tel Aviv's Exhibition Hall in 1937. The Philharmonic, considered one of the finest orchestras in the world, was founded by violinist Bronislaw Huberman in an attempt to counter Nazi propaganda against the Jews. He traveled around Poland and Germany, convincing the top Jewish musicians to come to Palestine and join the new orchestra. He then invited Toscanini to conduct the orchestra's premier concert. The sand dunes which led from Toscanini's lodgings to the Exhibition Hall were paved specially for this occasion.

The houses built in the 1920s and '30s were adorned with Hebrew motifs, which appeared on ceramic tiles designed in the workshops of Bezalel, the Jewish art academy in Jerusalem. Some of these tiles are still in place above the modern neon signs in Tel Aviv's busy shopping area and on street corners, providing the Hebrew name of the street.

The motifs were also incorporated into the plaster of the buildings' walls. The facade of the Herzliya Gymnasium, for example, was decorated with an illustration of the Temple in Jerusalem.

The Gymnasium's windows were large and shaped like keyholes, in the style of many ancient mosques; in the eyes of the architects, this design symbolized the union of the Western immigrants with their ancient roots in the East. These windows, as well as domes, bas-relief palm trees, and other such touches, can still be seen on many of Tel Aviv's houses.

Alongside the Mediterranean motifs, many modern design concepts such as the square Bauhaus style were introduced, as many young Jewish graduates of architectural schools all over the world moved to Tel Aviv.

American immigrants brought capital and business know-how to the city, and one of the more bizarre American projects was the casino erected on reinforced concrete columns dug into the bottom of the sea; it was the first time these concrete "stilts" had been used in the country. To accommodate the casino, Allenby Street, which started out parallel to the sea, was curved toward the beach, making the casino the last structure on the street.

In 1939 the casino was torn down because it blocked the view of the sea. Anyone walking along the seashore of Tel Aviv today might well wonder what became of the original concern for the view, now that the shore is lined with hotels that block the sea far more blatantly.

Americans also built the first commercial building, the Pinsk Mall, initiated by the American businessman Mordy Pinsk. The building, constructed in 1921, boasted Tel Aviv's first elevator, which was used only for cargo.

On May 14, 1948, the British Mandate for Palestine terminated. The provisional council of the representatives of the Jewish people in Israel assembled at the home of Mayor Dizengoff on Rothschild Boulevard. It was a solemn gathering. Seven Arab states had sworn to annihilate the as-yet-undeclared state if it dared to declare its independence.

Thousands of Tel Avivians gathered in the street in front of Dizengoff's house. People all over Israel and around the world listened in on their radio sets as the head of the provisional council, David Ben-Gurion, read aloud the Declaration of Independence of the State of Israel.

Tel Aviv, founded forty years earlier as a garden suburb, had been chosen as the city in which the birth of the State of Israel was officially announced.

The next day the Arab states invaded Israel in a direct act of war, although an unofficial war had been raging for many months between the Jews and Arabs of Palestine. The Arab armies set their sights on one distinct target: Tel Aviv. To them the conquest of Tel Aviv symbolized the conquest of modern Israel.

The inhabitants of Tel Aviv were under a severe strain, enduring sniper fire from the Arab town of Jaffa, attacks by Arabs from the surrounding villages, an air raid by the Egyptian Air Force, and an attempt by Egypt's naval force to reach the shores of Tel Aviv. The Egyptian army was stopped only 25 kilometers south of Tel Aviv, and ultimately the entire invasion was repelled.

At the end of the War of Independence, Tel Aviv became the main city of the new State of Israel and for a few years it was the seat of the government, until most administrative operations were moved to Jerusalem.

On April 24, 1950, Jaffa was incorporated into Tel Aviv and the city was officially called Tel Aviv-Jaffa. The city had come full circle from what began as a small suburb of Jaffa built by seekers of a little peace, quiet, and comfort in a garden setting away from the hustle and bustle of the ancient town.

The Judean Desert and Dead Sea

Just over the Judean Hills, to the east of Jerusalem, the Judean Desert abruptly begins. Suddenly there are no trees, the line of houses stops – and the traveler has entered the wilderness.

It is actually a local desert, not part of the global belt of deserts, and it is created by the Judean Hills which block it from the Mediterranean Sea. The sea air, after rising to the top of the hills 2,400 feet above sea level, then has to drop to the valley of the Dead Sea, 1,200 feet below sea level. The air stops cooling, does not vaporize into rain, and the result is a desert.

All is not bleak, however. Small springs deliver water in hidden canyons, and the runoff of rains from the top of the hills creates sudden flash floods in the dry river beds of the desert. A cloudburst now and then also supplies a little water. Those who can adapt to these conditions find the desert quite habitable.

Actually, man has always been drawn to the Judean Desert. Its desolate mountains and deep canyons made perfect hiding places for those in need of refuge. At the same time, its proximity to the populated areas of Judea and Samaria made it ideal for those who still wanted to keep an eye on the goings-on in civilization while pursuing the solitary life or "going underground."

The archaeologists probing its cliffs, mountains, caves and hiding places, have made startling discoveries. The search began quite accidentally.

In the autumn of 1947 a Bedouin shepherd lost some goats in a cave on the northwestern shore of the Dead Sea. Scrambling into the cave to get them out, he threw some stones into its darkest recesses – and heard a clinking sound. El Deib (The Wolf), as our shepherd was called, fled the cave in fright.

A few hours later he returned with a friend and some primitive torches to find out what had made that strange noise. There, in the furthest corner of the cave, he found that the stones he had thrown had hit some jars with lids on them. Upon opening them he found a leathery substance.

El Deib carefully removed the jars from the cave and several months later took them to Bethlehem to sell to an antique dealer. The merchant examined the contents of the jars and saw that the leather pieces had writing on them. He realized that they were ancient scrolls.

He paid the Bedouin for the items and told him to go and look for more and bring them back to him. He hurriedly telephoned a Jewish acquaintance, Prof. Sukenik of the Hebrew University of Jerusalem, telling him that he had some scrolls to show him.

It was now already the end of April 1948 and Jerusalem was caught up in the fighting between the Jews and Arabs as the British prepared to leave Palestine. Nevertheless, Sukenik agreed to meet the Arab antique dealer and, making his way through the fighting and the barbed wire, kept the rendezvous.

He looked at the scroll the dealer showed him. Carefully opening it a little, he saw Hebrew lettering on it which he recognized as dating back to the Roman period.

Sukenik was very excited and, meeting again with the dealer, he bought four of the scrolls.

This time, on opening one of them he found himself gazing at a 2,000-year-old scroll on which was inscribed the Book of Isaiah. He was overwhelmed.

That night, the State of Israel was proclaimed and Sukenik knew that the other three scrolls which the dealer had shown him – and which he still wanted to purchase – were now lost to him, out of reach across the border in Bethlehem.

At the time that the scrolls were purchased, the professor's son, Yigal Yadin, was commander-in-chief of the new Israel Defense Forces. When Yadin became a professor of archaeology in his own right, he bought the other three scrolls in a bizarre series of circumstances.

The scrolls had fallen into the hands of the Syrian Metropolitan, the head of the Syrian Church in Jerusalem, who had bought them from the antique dealer in Bethlehem. The Syrian Metropolitan emigrated, with the scrolls, to the United States, and advertised them in the Wall Street Journal. Yadin, who happened to be in New York, saw the ad and after secretly negotiating through a third party to conceal the fact that the potential buyer was the State of Israel, he succeeded in obtaining the scrolls.

Previous page: two views of the shoreline of the Dead Sea. Above: strange marl and clay formations carved by erosion into the ancient Dead Sea lake bed clay. Facing page: the sun-baked hills from Mizpeh Shalem, near the Dead Sea.

A few years after the State of Israel was born, all of the scrolls were in Jerusalem, on display at the Shrine of the Book, a special pavilion built for them at the Israel Museum.

Meanwhile, the Bedouins found out that cave-hunting was a lucrative business, and in the 1950s fragments of scrolls began appearing in the marketplaces of Jerusalem and Bethlehem. The Jordanian Department of Antiquities decided to investigate, and found the site of the original scrolls: the caves overlooking the Dead Sea at Khirbet Qumran.

The area was scientifically excavated and its full significance came to light. The archaeologists found the remains of a Jewish community that had lived on the shores of the Dead Sea from the first century BC to the first century AD.

A few ancient sources describe this community as the Essenes, who had decided to leave Jerusalem and lead a pure life in the desert in preparation for the coming of the Messiah, which they believed to be imminent. The community had special purification laws requiring, among other rites, numerous immersions in various ritual baths, which were discovered at the site.

The seven complete scrolls that had been found and the many thousands of scroll fragments which were now unearthed in the caves all belonged to the large library of the Essenes. When the Romans were about to destroy the community in reaction to the Jewish uprising in 66 AD, the Essenes hid the library in the nearby caves, where they lay unmolested for nearly 2,000 years.

The scrolls were inscribed with all of the books of the Bible except the book of Esther and are the oldest written Biblical accounts found to date. They are 1,000 years older than those previously found.

Other scrolls unearthed at Qumran dealt with the laws and rituals of the Essenes and still others contained apocryphal books of the Bible. A copper scroll discussed hidden treasures, and recently, the discovery of another scroll, which was hidden by the Bedouins and only sold much later, has been disclosed in a book by Yigal Yadin, who died a few days before the book was printed. This scroll provides a description of the Temple.

What has become apparent from the scrolls and finds, as well as other sources, is that the Essenes had ideas that were parallel to those of early Christianity. John the Baptist may have been influenced by the Essenes and, at one point in his life, may even have been belonged to the community.

After the area of Qumran was more thoroughly excavated, scrolls and ancient remains again began to appear in the marketplace. The archaeologists, still following the Bedouins, who were now experts in finding historic remains – reached another set of caves in an even more remote desert canyon. Excavating at the site, they uncovered letters written by Bar Kochba, the legendary commander of the second Jewish uprising against the Romans in 132-135 AD.

These documents had probably been hidden by the people living in the Dead Sea area when they realized that the Romans were approaching. The residents themselves hid in the caves as well and eventually died there.

With the creation of the State of Israel, the Judean Desert and the Dead Sea were divided between Israel and Jordan. For the Bedouins, the scavengers of the desert, ceasefire lines and world politics had no meaning. Once their caches, on the Jordanian side of the ceasefire line, were all depleted, they crossed over and searched for finds on the Israeli side.

The Israeli archaeologists decided on a different plan of action from that of their Jordanian colleagues. Instead of following the Bedouins to the finds, they would conduct an expedition systematically to search each canyon, cliff face, cave and hidden rock cleft.

In the years 1961-1962, teams of archaeologists, Israel Defense Forces personnel and volunteers painstakingly combed the desert. At the very outset of the search, in a cave in Nahal Mishmar, a treasure was found: over 400 pieces of beautifully worked bronze. They belonged to the Chalcolithic Age (4,000-2,200 BC) and may have been the utensils used in an empty Chalcolithic temple found in Ein-Gedi.

The bronze hoard illuminated a very obscure period, the beginning of civilization, when a group of people suddenly arrived in the area with a sophisticated technology for smelting bronze and carving ivory and just as suddenly packed their belongings and disappeared from history.

The finely crafted pieces are permanently displayed at the Israel Museum in Jerusalem.

Even more dramatic finds were still awaiting the searchers. On a cliff top, overlooking the deep ravine of Nahal Hever, lay the remains of two Roman army camps, one on each side of the ravine. The camps were built on top of a group of caves to prevent the escape of the last holdouts of the Bar Kochba uprising, who had hidden themselves in the caves. All the Romans had to do was wait. Either the rebels would die of thirst and starvation or they would come out and be caught.

In 1953, the first dig was conducted at the site. Originally, a narrow ledge had provided access to the small openings of the caves in the cliff face, but it had long since collapsed, so the members of the expedition had to make their way into the caves by means of ropes and ladders. The expedition uncovered a few remains from the Bar Kochba uprising.

In 1961, a more thorough search was organized in order to excavate the caves completely. In one of the caves, later dubbed the Cave of Horrors, a group of skulls and bones enclosed in a palm-frond basket greeted the startled explorers. The dryness of the desert had helped preserve the remains and, as the search went on, clothing, baskets, wooden utensils and many more items were uncovered intact.

In another cave, called the Cave of the Letters, a fascinating collection of artifacts was found very close to the surface. Awaiting the archaeologists were bronze jugs and utensils, glass plates still packed in their palm-frond wrappings, clothing, knitting material, and even the keys to the rebels' houses, which they had left locked in the hope of being able to return home after the Romans had departed.

Two groups of documents provided a vivid picture of everyday life around the Dead Sea in the second century. One was a batch of letters written to "Joshua, Son of Golgala," the commander of the rebellion in the Dead Sea area, by his commander-in-chief, "Shimon Bar Kosiba – the President of Israel." Here were letters written by a legendary rebel leader whose exact name had never been known!

The other group of documents was found in a little leather bag. They belonged to a Jewish woman named "Babta, daughter of Shimon," who had married at least twice and had children and property from each of her marriages. She owned a great deal of real estate around the Dead Sea.

Babta was in the process of suing her first husband's family for custodianship of her

These pages: the ruins of Masada, high above the Dead Sea. The elaborate palaces and fortifications were built by Herod the Great, but are best known as a stronghold of Jewish zealots in their resistance to the Romans in 72-73 A.D.

young daughter's property and consequently had to appear in court in Ein-Gedi, bringing with her all of her papers: marriage certificates, legal agreements with her former family, deeds to her property, property tax certificates and many other documents. She had efficiently organized them in groups, enclosing each group in a separate wrapper so that it would be easy to find.

We know much more about Babta today than she would have divulged about herself when she was alive. We even know, nearly 2,000 years later, that she owned more property than she declared to the tax authorities.

She was probably not one of the rebels, though a relative of her former husband was Joshua, Son of Golgala, the commander of the uprising in the Dead Sea area. Rather than waste her breath trying to explain her presence in Ein Gedi to the Romans, however, she chose to hide in the cave with the rebels.

The excavation of Masada provided further archaeological bounty. Masada is a rock with cliff faces on which King Herod built himself a palace and fortress in the first century BC. It was to be a refuge for the king if he was ever deposed by the Romans or rebelled against by his subjects.

Herod invested tremendous effort in making the place liveable and defensible. An ingenious water supply system was devised, utilizing the flash floods in the surrounding areas. Storehouses for food and weapons were built, as well as villas, palaces, workshops and even a swimming pool.

He never needed the palace, though, and after he died it became a Roman garrison. At the beginning of the first revolt of the Jews against the Romans in 66 AD it was taken in a surprise attack by the Jewish forces. They opened its arsenal and used the weapons for the storming of Jerusalem.

The fighters who had taken Masada were extremists who were subsequently expelled from Jerusalem by their fellow Jews and returned to Masada. They were called the Sicarii (the people of the little daggers) and were led by Elazar Ben Yair.

The Jewish historian Josephus, who lived in that period and witnessed the uprising, described the events at Masada.

Josephus related that after the destruction of the Temple in Jerusalem the revolt was quashed, and the only Jewish fighters to remain at large were scattered in three fortresses in the Judean Desert: Herodion, Macheraeus, and Masada. In 73 AD, three years after the end of the rebellion, the Romans decided to destroy all remnants of the Jewish resistance.

They promptly captured Herodion and Macheraeus, and then arrived at Masada, where they built a wall around the fortress with eight camps deployed alongside it. They then erected a ramp leading up the rock, in order to roll their battering ram up to the fortress and break through its walls.

A whole legion and auxiliary forces were camped around Masada, about 5,000 strong. On top of the mountain 960 people, including women and children, desperately struggled to withstand the siege. It was just a matter of time before the Roman forces would burst into the fortress and capture the defenders.

According to Josephus's account, once the ramp had been built and the walls had begun to crumble from the repeated thrusts of the battering ram, the commander of the fortress, Elazar Ben Yair, persuaded the defenders to end their lives rather than fall prisoner to the Romans.

Each man killed his own family, and lots were drawn for ten men to kill the heads of the families. Of the ten remaining men one was chosen, again by lot, to kill all of the others, and the last man eventually committed suicide. When the Romans entered the fortress the next day they were met by a ghostly silence and a gory scene.

This narrative ended Josephus's book *The Jewish Wars*. For him the story of Masada conveyed an important message for all Jews: striving for Jewish independence is a suicidal act. The result is only death and destruction.

Today, 1,912 years later, Masada is a national park in the independent State of Israel.

Facing page: ruins of Masada. When the Romans seemed certain to break into the fortress of Masada in 73 A.D., the zealot leader Elazar ben Yair persuaded his followers to kill each other in order to cheat the Romans of victory. Only seven Jews, who hid during the slaughter, survived to tell the tale of the zealots' ultimate sacrifice.

Life in the Wilderness

The Jews of ancient times grew date palms on the shores of the Dead Sea and in the oasis of Jericho. They also raised the *afarsemon*, whose literal translation is "persimmon" but was apparently an enigmatic tropical bush whose fruit had pharmaceutical properties. What was even more interesting about the afarsemon was that it was considered a very powerful aphrodisiac.

The farming of the afarsemon – perhaps the modern balsam plant – was a secret passed from father to son, and the afarsemon fields were ardently coveted by the rulers of the land, who made the areas of cultivation part of their domain.

During the Jewish uprisings the Romans had to contend with the Jewish farmers, who uprooted their own bushes in an early version of civil disobedience.

In the oasis of Ein Gedi a synagogue from the Roman period has been excavated. An inscription in its floor places a terrible curse on anyone who divulges to an outsider the secret of growing the afarsemon – "the secret of the community," as it is worded in the inscription.

The Dead Sea itself was exploited for asphalt, which was used for embalming purposes; it was exported to Egypt for the mummification process.

After the Romans fell from power all of this agricultural and industrial activity ended, and the Dead Sea area and the Judean Desert became a wilderness once more.

For a few decades, monks and hermits dwelled in its caves and canyons, building monasteries and churches in remote locations. Famous saints, like Sabas and Khariton, founded abbeys and other retreats. During the fourth and fifth centuries the desert teemed with ascetics and with pilgrims who made their way from monastery to monastery to visit these pious men who had moved out to the desert to be closer to God and to find solitude.

At the beginning of the first century AD, with the collapse of Byzantine rule and Persian and Arab conquest, this community, too, came to an end, and the area returned to its former desolation.

Today's Dead Sea, simmering in the heat of the Lower Jordan Valley, is still characterized by desert extremes. At 1,200 feet below sea level, it is the lowest point on earth, and with a salt content of 32% it is the saltiest body of water in the world. The average air temperature is over 110 degrees Fahrenheit and can peak at over 120 degrees, with relatively little humidity. Needless to say, the Dead Sea is quite dead.

What the Dead Sea can boast, however, is huge mineral reserves. In it are potash, one of the chief components of chemical fertilizer; bromine, an important agent in the manufacture of the various fuel octanes; and metal magnesium, a very light metal used in many of the most sophisticated industries.

When Theodore Herzl wrote his utopian novel *Altneuland*, about the Jewish state, he described in detail the industries he envisioned on the shores of the Dead Sea, processing the mineral wealth of the new nation.

Herzl never visited the Dead Sea because access to its shores was too difficult. If he had ventured out there and encountered the debilitating climate perhaps even he would have given up his dream for the area.

One of the readers of Herzl's novel was a Jewish mining engineer from Siberia, A.M. Novomeisky. He decided to go to the Dead Sea and find out for himself if the chemicals there could really be mined. Even before going there he began negotiating, in 1906, with the World Zionist Organization for the construction of a chemical plant on the Dead Sea shore.

In 1911 he visited the Dead Sea and began his experiments. It did not take him long to conclude that the minerals in the Dead Sea could be extracted from the water by evaporation, a very easy process in one of the hottest corners of the world. He decided, therefore, to try to extract potash by means of a system of evaporation ponds. Novomeisky's experiments meant that the Dead Sea plant would be the first modern plant in the world to be powered by solar energy.

Above: a modern sculpture on the shores of the Dead Sea, near Masada.

Above: 1,296 feet above the Dead Sea stands this sign, which marks true sea level.

In 1920, upon the conclusion of World War I, Novomeisky resumed his experiments and began negotiating with the British mandatory authorities for a concession to mine potash from the Dead Sea. The British kept him waiting ten years, sometimes out of sheer bureaucracy and sometimes in response to criticism from business circles in Britain which disapproved of the granting of concessions to non-Britons.

Novomeisky had to submit the results of his meticulous Dead Sea research to the authorities. They proceeded to make his findings public in 1925 and to include them in each copy of the tender that was issued for the rights to the concession.

The publication of Novomeisky's work and the issuance of the tender provoked a clamorous competition for the concession, with American, Australian, and British companies among the chief rivals. In 1927 the British granted the concession jointly to

Novomeisky and to Major Tolock, a Briton who had never been to Palestine but had written a memorandum to the British government in 1918 requesting a concession to mine the Dead Sea.

Now, however, the British placed another obstacle in Novomeisky's path: he had to prove that he had the funds to build the plant, and the idealistic but frustrated mining engineer had to run from company to company and from organization to organization trying to raise the money, while his British partner sat by and did nothing.

In 1929 the British finally released the concession to Novomeisky. Forty-seven percent of the company's income, plus five percent of the minerals mined, was to go to the government. The concession was for a period of seventy-five years – that is, until the year 2005 – and then the company and its property would revert back to the government.

The plant went into operation in 1932 and began exporting bromine and potash. It was a huge pioneering project which was a magnet for all those who wanted to prove the possibility of creating a modern Jewish state in the land of Israel.

In 1934 a second plant was opened in the southern part of the Dead Sea, in Sodom; the Sodom made famous by Lot and his family. The only access to that plant was by boat.

Near the northern plant, a few Jewish settlers decided to attempt to establish an agricultural farm. They washed the salt off the soil and began to plant dates and raise livestock.

With the outbreak of the War of Independence, the northern plant fell into Jordanian hands. The new proprietors looted the factory and machinery and the plant has lain derelict ever since. The southern plant was cut off from the rest of the country at the beginning of the fighting, but after withstanding attacks and isolation it was reached by the Israel Defense Forces, who utilized an old Roman road to get to the southern part of the Dead Sea.

Today, the southern plant is the biggest chemical enterprise in Israel and one of the largest of its kind in the world. For the past few years the Jordanians have been building a plant on their side of the Dead Sea.

The latest developments on the Dead Sea are solar ponds, which utilize the heat of the sun and the salinity of the Dead Sea's water to create cheap, solar energy.

Six farming communities, "kibbutzim," produce dates and other agricultural products along the shores of the Dead Sea, and many hotels and resorts have been established, taking advantage of the health benefits of the mineral-rich water.

The Judean Desert is a large nature reserve where the wildlife of the desert has rejuvenated itself to the delight of hikers and other visitors.

The Dead Sea and the Judean Desert have once again opened for business, and Babta, the shrewd property owner, would be counting her acres greedily if she was alive today.

The Galilee

Israel's north, the Galilee, is the fertile part of the country. Abundant winter rains create a green covering for its mountains and valleys.

The mountains of the Galilee are divided into two major groups. The first, the mountains of Upper Galilee, reach a height of 3,600 feet. They begin in Lebanon and extend into northern Israel, ending in a cliff beyond which stands the second group, the mountains of Lower Galilee. Only 1,800 feet high, this second group is comprised of a series of parallel mountain ranges and fertile valleys.

Above: detail, remains of ruined Second Temple period synagogue, whose excavation helped to establish that modern Kfar Nahum was the biblical Capernaum.

The Galilee is surrounded on three sides by plains: the coastal plain to the west, the Jezreel, Harod, and Beit Shean valleys to the south, and the Hula and Jordan River valleys to the east. To the far north of the Galilee are the headwaters of the Jordan River, fed by the snows of Mount Hermon, which rises east of the Galilee to over 10,000 feet above sea level.

The Jordan River flows through the Hula Valley and the Jordan River Valley, a deep valley formed by a rift in the face of the earth that is over 6,000 kms long and runs from Turkey to Ethiopia. In this rift is the lowest point on earth, the Dead Sea, 1,200 feet below sea level, but in the Galilee the rift is only 600 feet below sea level.

Three lakes are formed by the river: the Hula Lake, or the "Upper Waters," as it is called in the Bible, a former swamp that has been drained and transformed into fertile farmland; the Sea of Galilee, a little futher south, and the Dead Sea.

The plain of Jezreel has seen human habitation for many thousands of years. Its ancient center was Megiddo, where archaeological excavations have uncovered over twenty different layers of cities dating back nearly 2,000 years.

The Galilee's mountains, however, are its true center, inhabited by humans all the way back to prehistoric man, whose remains have been found in various caves.

The home of the tribes of Asher, Zevulun, Naphtali, and Issachar, the Galilee was a wild, rocky, forested region until humankind settled in. Hardy folk lived in the Galilee – farmers and shepherds whose only concern was to work the land and tend to their livestock. The arrival of the Romans shattered that insular existence. Wars, famine, and heavy taxation roused many of the inhabitants to action and consequently, from 55 BC to 73 AD, the Galilee gave birth to two distinct ideas for remedying the situation.

One, propounded by a newly established Jewish extremist party, asserted that only complete political independence for the Jews was the answer. The partisans, led by Josephus in the Galilee, rose up against the Romans all over the country, perpetrating acts of terrorism and fighting pitched battles from nooks and crannies and from mountain fortresses.

The Romans responded brutally, and finally launched an all-out war in 66 AD, destroying cities and strongholds. Gamla, Yodfat, Tzipori, Magdal and other fortresses were among the battlefronts. By 70 AD the Romans had succeeded in quelling the Jewish rebellion (aside from a few last strongholds in Masada and the desert, all of which fell by 73 AD).

While the Jews were beginning to agitate against the Romans, a young man from the little village of Nazareth in the Galilee set out on a fateful journey. It would take him through the towns and villages of the Galilee to the Sea of Galilee – and finally to Jerusalem. Jesus of Nazareth carried a message of love and peace, proclaiming that war and destruction were not the paths of redemption.

Commencing his ministry in Nazareth, Jesus moved to the shores of the Sea of Galilee, where for three years he brought his message to the fishermen and farmers of the Galilee. Word spread through the villages of the north and many flocked to hear Jesus' teachings.

A new concept was born: the notion that it mattered little who ruled the country. What was important was to worship one's God. ("Give to Caesar what is Caesar's and to God what is God's" – Mark 12:17)

Although the rebels and Jesus' followers were keenly aware of the issues, most Galileans were perplexed by these messages and continued to adhere to their traditional ways.

With the Roman destruction of the centers of Jewish learning around Jerusalem, the Galilee became the focus of Jewish life, the place where the rabbis taught, commented, and edited that great body of Jewish law, the Jerusalem Talmud.

Previous pages: Mount Carmel affords an ideal viewpoint overlooking Haifa.

Facing page: the Church of the Primacy of Peter on the shores of the Sea of Galilee, the site where Jesus gave Peter the office of Primacy.

Synagogues sprang up in every little village and the villagers strove to create their own autonomous Jewish communities.

Meanwhile, the Roman/Byzantine Empire became Christian and in the Galilee – the home of Jesus – churches, shrines, and monasteries began to appear.

The rise of the area's population brought with it an economic boom, but decline was imminent. The Byzantine Empire was brought to its knees in 636 by the Arab invasion. The Galilee was no exception. The fall was not immediate, but rather a process of insidious deterioration.

The Crusaders came and went, after battling the forces of Islam across the mountains of Galilee. Fortresses like Belvoir, Montfort, Beaufort, St. Jean D'Acre, Chastelet and Chastel Neuf are the legacies of these brave soldiers. Saladin finally defeated the Crusaders conclusively in 1187, in the battle of the Horns of Hittim.

With the departure of the Crusaders, the Galilee was all but forgotten.

In 1516 the Ottoman Turks defeated the Egyptian Mamelukes and as a result the whole region, including the Galilee, became part of the Ottoman Empire.

The regional capital was Safed (Zefat), a little town on a plateau. Above it stand the remains of a Crusader castle.

For nearly a hundred years Safed was to be one of the most important centers of Judaism – or to be more precise, Jewish mysticism. A few years before, in 1492, the Jews had been expelled from the main center of Jewish life in that era – Spain.

Many of the expellees found refuge in the new and rapidly expanding Ottoman Empire, where their political, financial and administrative acumen made them very useful to the Turkish authorities. Under these favorable conditions some Jews migrated to Safed and established a weaving and dying industry there.

Jewish mystics and scholars also began to migrate to Safed. According to tradition, the Galilee had been the home of the early Jewish mystics of the Roman period – especially Rabbi Shimon Bar Yochai, buried on Mount Meron near Safed. He was thought to be the author of the most important source on Jewish mysticism, the *Zohar* (Splendor).

The new arrivals in Safed made their own contribution to Jewish tradition. Rabbi Joseph Caro wrote *Shulchan Aruch* (The Set Table), a book codifying Jewish religious practice. Rabbi Shlomo Halevi Alkabetz arrived in the city from Saloniki and taught there; he composed many prayers, the most famous of which was "Lecha Dodi" (Come my beloved), which is sung in every synagogue on the eve of the Sabbath.

The best-known figure was undoubtedly HaAri (The Lion) – an acronym for "our teacher Rabbi Isaac". His full name was Rabbi Isaac Ashkenazi Luria. He was born, grew up, and taught in Egypt, though his legendary birthplace was Jerusalem.

The pull of the mystical center in Safed was very powerful and he emigrated there to study and teach the philosophy of mysticism. Many students from all over the world gathered around him, and were called the "lion cubs." After his untimely death his students carried on his work.

Facing page: the ruins of the Moslem-built
Nimrod's Castle, which was subsequently used by
the Crusaders.

Rabbi Luria arranged the Sabbath liturgy as we know it today. Every Friday, dressed in white, he and his disciples would walk together towards the East to meet the Sabbath bride. Today, when "Lecha Dodi" is sung in the synagogue, at the last verse the singers turn toward the door to meet the Sabbath bride, as Rabbi Luria and his students did in the sixteenth century in Safed.

Left: in its setting overlooking the sea stands the white-domed tomb of Rabbi Meir Baal Haness. Facing page: Fisherman's Harbor in Acre. Below: the Sea of Galilee is firmly fixed in the minds of many people as the place where Jesus' Miracle of the Loaves and Fishes took place, commemorated in this mosaic in Tabgha. Overleaf: the modern face of Nazareth, Jesus' childhood home, showing the conical roof of the Roman Catholic Church of the Annunciation, completed in 1966 on the site of a Crusader foundation.

Safed's fame was not to last long and at the end of the sixteenth century the Galilee lapsed back into obscurity. A small Jewish population continued to live in the city, however, and in 1878 a group of Jewish families left Safed to become farmers. They bought plots of land in the village of Jeoni in the Hula Valley and launched their agricultural enterprise.

They had no experience whatsoever in farming, and after three difficult, drought-stricken years, the settlement disintegrated. Of the 150 original settlers only three families remained, living from what they could glean from the Arab farmers.

The farmers were harassed in their hometown of Safed, and became outcasts. According to the townsfolk, Jews were meant to study and pray, not to work the land.

Some Jews thought otherwise, however, and in 1882 a new group of Jewish settlers arrived in the Galilee. A few years earlier, in their native Rumania, they had created a cooperative for the settlement of Palestine. They were part of a movement called "Lovers of Zion," dedicated to the rebirth of a new Jewish nation in its ancient homeland.

These immigrants settled on land purchased from the earlier Jewish settlers. They called their settlement Rosh Pina (The Cornerstone), from Psalms 118:22: "A stone abandoned by the builders shall become a cornerstone."

For the first few years the settlement barely survived, and would have gone bankrupt

had it not been for the aid provided by Baron Edmund de Rothschild, who played a major part in developing and helping new Jewish settlements in Palestine.

The farmers tried many experiments in their early agricultural efforts. In one of them, mulberry seeds and silkworms were imported from the mountains of the Himalayas and a silk industry was created in Rosh Pina. By 1900 there were over 1,500 acres of mulberry trees in Palestine.

The dumping of cheap silk from China and Japan on the world market, and incessant squabbling between the workers and management of the silk factory, brought the Galilee silk industry to ruin.

The Jews continued to develop the Galilee despite numerous obstacles and by World War I many Jewish settlements were functioning there, including seven in the Hula Valley and three on the Golan Heights.

In 1920 a tragic and momentous drama occurred on the northernmost tip of the Galilee.

As the Turks retreated from the Galilee in the aftermath of World War I, the British did not advance further north than Rosh Pina, since they had divided the area between themselves and the French. The French army, which had landed in Beirut, was not yet ready to advance inland.

Into the vacuum thus created stepped the Amir Feisal, Arab ally of the British, who had assisted the British war effort in its final stages and had been promised an Arab state in return.

He marched into Damascus, which the Turks had abandoned, and declared it the capital of his Arab state. The French objected, as Damascus had been promised to them, and marched on the city. Feisal managed to rule in Damascus for a few short months, though, and his forces and local Arab soldiers decided to clear the area of all non-Arab settlements.

Four Jewish settlements in the north, with a little over 200 settlers, were affected. The majority of the settlers immediately fled to Beirut, but two kibbutzim decided to hold out: Kfar Giladi and Tel-Hai (The Hill of Life).

The settlers called for reinforcements from the southern Jewish settlements, but immediate aid was not forthcoming since none of them had formal defense organizations. One man did arrive – Joseph Trumpeldor – who had been a captain in the Russian army. He had lost an arm in the Russo-Japanese War of 1905 and had been decorated by the Czar for bravery, though the Czar was surprised to learn, at the decoration ceremony, that the war hero was Jewish.

Trumpeldor had decided to devote himself to organizing Jewish settlement in Palestine. During World War I he organized the Jewish Mule Corps in the British Army. After the war he arrived in Palestine and heard of the call for help from the Jewish settlers in the Galilee.

For over three months the two settlements at the tip of the Galilee held out, isolated and with few weapons and little ammunition. On March 1, 1920, the Arabs attacked again. This time they arrived at the settlement and demanded entry to check if there were any French officers inside. The settlers admitted a few officers and troops. Once inside, the attackers searched the building and holed up in one of the rooms, the only room on the second floor of the complex.

Killing the two men and two women in the room, the Arabs opened fire from inside the settlement simultaneously. The attack lasted the whole day. After a few hours, the Arab officer in charge inside asked permission to leave, saying that the attack had all been a misunderstanding and that he would calm the troops outside. The defenders, unaware that the four had been killed, allowed the Arabs to leave.

The attack continued, but the settlers held out, and by evening the Arabs had withdrawn. Seven people had been killed and a few wounded, including Trumpeldor. With so few defenders left to hold the position, it was decided to retreat to Kfar Giladi.

They set fire to their home and began to climb to Kfar Giladi. Halfway up the hill, Trumpeldor died. His last words were in Latin, spoken to the doctor who was among the defenders: "It is good to die for our country!"

That night all those assembled at Kfar Giladi decided to abandon that settlement as well and retreat to the south. On their way south they met the reinforcements which had finally been sent from the southern settlements.

The battle and the death of the eight settlers was not in vain. It became a symbol of Jews defending themselves, and one of its lessons was the need to create a Jewish defense force. In 1920 the Haganah (Defense) military organization was created and in 1948 it became the Israel Defense Forces.

A year after the battle of Tel-Hai, the defenders returned to their settlements because the area had been included in the mandate given to the British by the League of Nations. The French forces ousted Feisal from Damascus and received a mandate to govern Syria and Lebanon.

Jewish settlements were established all over the Galilee. After Israel's War of Independence, Kiryat Shemona (The Town of the Eight) was built; it was named in memory of the eight Jewish defenders who died at Tel-Hai.

Trumpeldor and his comrades are buried under the statue of a roaring lion in Kfar Giladi, overlooking the hills and valleys of the Galilee. Inscribed on the statue are Trumpeldor's last words: "It is good to die for our country!"

Previous page: a sun-drenched field of poppies by the roadside. Facing page: the miracle of

Cana as portrayed in the Franciscan Church at Kfar Kana. Above: views of Galilee wildlife.

The Negev

Over half of Israel is comprised of a desert, with an average rainfall of under 10 inches per year, most parts receiving under 6 inches annually and some under an inch.

Carved out by wind and water over the eons, desert landscapes are probably the most striking sights in any land. Israel's desert, the Negev, is no exception.

The Negev consists of several sections. In the north, around Beer Sheva, lie flatlands. To the south is a series of mountain ranges divided by deep valleys.

Atop five of these ranges are *machteshim*, a Hebrew term for unique geomorphological phenomena: crater-like formations which provide a window into the geological history of the earth's crust. Each machtesh is spectacular in its own way.

Southwest of these mountain ranges is the large Avdat Plateau, crossed by one of the biggest wadis (dry riverbeds) in the Negev, Nahal Zin.

Facing page: one of the natural arches, and (above) the 'mushroom,' natural rock formations located in Machtesh Timna, a nature reserve north of Eilat.

The appearance of a wadi can be deceptive. Though it looks at first as if it was never touched by a drop of water, closer scrutiny reveals canyons, the markings of dry waterfalls, water holes, and, if you keep walking, small local springs, a green line of bushes, and sometimes even small trees, which could not have sprung up without water.

And if you happen to be caught in a wadi on a rainy day, you find out just how much water can flow through it. When the rain falls on the dry, barren, soilless ground of the desert, it keeps right on going, quickly finding an outlet in the wadis and gathering to create a raging torrent. Water can flow through Nahal Zin and Nahal Paran for three to five days after a rainfall.

For the unwary traveler this sudden wall of water can be an extremely unpleasant surprise. Anything in the vicinity of the wadi can be washed away, including roads, bridges, and heavy vehicles.

Above left: the Somali wild ass and (above right) the familiar camel, both creatures of the desert. Facing page: the tombs of David Ben-Gurion, under whose leadership the State of Israel was established and who continued to lead the new nation for nearly two decades, and his wife Paula, at Sde Boker in the Negev, where they spent the last years of their lives.

The Avdat Plateau gives way in the south to the highlands – remote, forbidding mountains, rarely traversed by human beings. To the east of the Negev lies the Arava Valley, continuing down from the Jordan Valley along the Syrian-African Rift which extends from Lebanon to Ethiopia. The plateau of northern Sinai merges into the Negev from the west and the granite Arabo-Nubian Massif which makes up the mountains of Sinai juts up into the southern Negev. At the southernmost tip of the Negev is the Gulf of Eilat, or Aqaba, which is an offshoot of the Red Sea.

Life exists in the Negev, but, as in any desert, habitation requires resourceful adaptation to its conditions. Water conservation is the main issue for an organism trying to survive.

Most of the animals that inhabit the Negev endure by hiding during the day and emerging at night, secreting very little water, benefiting from various anatomical cooling systems, and in many other instinctive and physiological ways. The camel and the goat, for example, have unique metabolisms which allow them to absorb large amounts of water in a very short time when they need to compensate quickly for water loss.

Plants are structured even more ingeniously to conserve water.

Human beings who have tried to survive in the desert have had to use their intelligence to adapt to conditions of water scarcity.

Prehistoric Negev dwellers experienced a different climate: the Ice Age in Europe was not quite over and the Negev was a vast grassland. These early residents hunted wild animals and made flint blocks – and migrated when the climate changed.

Right and above right: the modern Ben-Gurion University of the Negev in Beersheva. Above: the 5th century church in the Nabatean city of Avdat. The Nabateans were an ancient people of the region who came to prominence as the Seleucid kingdom crumbled after 200 B.C., but who lost their independence to Rome in 106 A.D. Facing page: a reconstructed Nabatean farm, built near Avdat to prove the efficiency of Nabatean methods of farming in the arid Negev.

Since the dawn of history the Negev has been a desert. Abraham wandered through it as he made his way from Canaan to Egypt and back again. Hagar, his concubine, was cast out of Abraham's tent by his wife Sarah, and after plodding along in the desert with her son Ishmael she finally collapsed under a bush – and was miraculously supplied with water. She called the lifesaving well Be'er Lehai Ro'i (Well of the One Who Lives and Sees). Through the Negev trudged the people of Israel on their exodus from Egypt, and along its dusty trail the prophet Elijah went to the mountain of God, Horev.

The biblical sources tell us of a few of the kings of Judea who managed to settle the Negev, and archaeological excavations have uncovered a whole system of roads, fortifications, and water cisterns that date back to the tenth to sixth century BC.

Five ghost towns of the Nabateans from the Greek and Roman periods – Nitzana, Mamshit, Haluza, Shivta, and Avdat – offer the most profuse evidence of human

habitation during the Negev's early desert period. Most of the houses, streets, markets, and churches of these towns have remained intact. Surrounding the towns were acres and acres of farmland.

The Nabateans mastered the secrets of the desert. Migrating from Arabia and Edom, they established themselves as traders and transporters of spices from Arabia to the Mediterranean coast, along the desert paths of the Negev.

By terracing and claiming the dry riverbeds, the Nabateans turned the wadis into fertile fields and farmed the barren hills for water. The hills and mountains had channels around them which conducted all rain to the place where the water was needed. They collected the 10-inch annual rainfall from an area ten times the size of the plot being irrigated, so that they could make use of nearly 100 inches of rain.

The Nabateans originally had their own religion. Then they became Hellenized, worshipping the gods of the Eastern Hellenistic world, and finally, at the zenith of their civilization, became Christian. Shivta, for example, a small town on the western edge of the Negev, had two large churches and a monastery.

In the seventh century the Moslems attacked from Arabia. Under Moslem rule the economic system broke down and the Negev towns were gradually abandoned. By the ninth or tenth century the nomads could roam freely across the desert once again.

These herdsmen would wander over large areas of desert, organized in clans and tribes and living in tents made of camel hair. They were – and are – much more than just exotic "local color" in picturesque encampments. They are the fathers of the desert, returning time after time in the retreating footsteps of civilization.

Today, modern Israel is rolling the desert back. By piping in water from the north and utilizing the most sophisticated agricultural technology possible, Israeli planners and scientists have found a way to make the Negev habitable for more and more people and industries.

Above: with their camel and other possessions,
an Arab family makes its way along the shores
of the Gulf of Eilat.

Beer Sheva, a city of 130,000 people, once stood at the center of the Negev; today it is the desert's northern portal. Barren landscapes once accompanied the traveler to Beer Sheva from the north; now green fields have spread southward. Eilat, Mitzpe Ramon, Sde Boker, and many more settlements dot the Negev with outposts of advanced civilization.

The Desert Research Institute of the University of the Negev in Beer Sheva is studying new ways to adapt to desert living. Phosphates and a few other minerals are being mined in the Negev.

Above: romantic, historic ruins of the Crusader castle on Coral Island in the Red Sea, south of Eilat.

With the growing conquest of the elements, civilization is taking over the desert landscapes to such a degree that it is in danger of harming the natural beauty and delicate ecology of the desert.

Preventative measures have been taken, however. In the past twenty years, large nature reserves have been designated and stringent conservation laws have been enacted, and the Nature Reserves Authority has been created to guard and maintain the balance between the desert's ecology and adaptation to human habitation.

In addition, a network of trails and paths has been marked in the nature reserves, and ancient sites and monuments have been restored.

Since the return of the Sinai to the Egyptians, the Negev is one of the few areas where one can still take refuge from the stress and strain of everyday life, become enveloped in the wilderness and the big sky, and walk for days along desert trails without coming into contact with civilization.

It is hoped that the delicate balance between development and preservation will be maintained so that both civilization and wildlife will continue to flourish in the Negev.

Modern Israel

Though Jews had always lived in the Holy Land, by the Middle Ages their numbers had dwindled considerably. Unstable conditions, a shattered economy, and a subsistence-level existence had driven them out of the country. Greener pastures beckoned in the Diaspora.

Though the Jews sang "Next Year in Jerusalem" every Passover and prayed for the rebirth of the nation in its own land, they were referring to the time after the coming of the Messiah, not the present. They believed that they should not force the Messiah's hand by a premature return.

The few Jewish travelers who visited the Holy Land reported on the difficult conditions while they toured the country's holy sites, burial places of rabbis and sages, synagogues, and Jewish communities, mainly in the four holy cities of Safed, Tiberias, Hebron, and Jerusalem.

In the 1880s a change came about which signalled the beginning of modern Israel. For various reasons Jews around the world, but mainly those in Eastern Europe, began to think about going back to the Holy Land and reviving the nation of Israel.

The end of the nineteenth century was a period when new states were founded, and many people fought for and obtained their independence, but for the Jewish people the situation was not so clear-cut. They had difficulty fitting themselves in with the new nationalism – were they part of the new Polish, Rumanian, German, Greek, Austrian nation? Or did they constitute a nation by themselves?

An answer to this question was forced on many of them when they were not accepted as full partners in the new order. A good number of them had been staunch fighters for these changes and they were shocked and grieved by this rebuff. Many looked across the ocean to the new nation whose constitution was based on the principles of equality and democracy, and they left in the biggest Jewish exodus ever witnessed: emigration to the United States.

Millions poured out of Eastern Europe, uprooting themselves to make the long and difficult voyage to the New World. Some stayed behind in Europe, trying to come to terms with their situation, and a few decided that it was time to rebuild the Jewish nation in its ancient homeland.

These "Lovers of Zion," as they were called, formed groups to prepare for their return to the land. In 1883 they began arriving in Palestine, town folk with families and a little money who wanted to be farmers in order to build up the land for the Jewish people. With scant knowledge of the country or of farming they bought land – mainly agriculturally useless plots – and tried to cultivate it.

The first of their new settlements was called Rishon LeZion (The First to Zion) and was situated in the wastelands to the south of Jaffa.

The founding families paid a great deal of money for the land and then spent another substantial sum to dig a well. Their funds were rapidly running out, but help was to come from an unexpected quarter. Baron Edmund de Rothschild of France, for reasons still unclear, decided to come to the rescue of Rishon LeZion and its sister settlements.

Facing page: Hall of Remembrance at Yad Vashem, a memorial to the millions of Jews murdered in the Holocaust.

He spent enormous amounts of money to put the settlements on their feet, bringing in experts to teach and study the agricultural aspects of the land, experimenting with new industries, buying more land, and building more settlements.

The Baron also created a bureaucracy to help and guide the settlers, and this administrative machinery quickly took control of their lives and eventually stifled all creativity and idealism. What had started as a dream of a new Jewish nation had been diluted into a quiet, controlled life as farm owners in the Holy Land.

The settlers of the late nineteenth century were called the First Aliyah (the first wave of immigration) and each new group of arrivals was referred to in this chronological fashion. Each left its distinctive mark on the country they eventually helped transform into a state.

In 1897 Theodore Herzl, a Viennese Jewish journalist, convened the first Zionist Congress. A few years earlier he had been harshly made aware of the problems of Jewish life in Europe while covering the trial of a French army officer, Alfred Dreyfus. Dreyfus was accused of divulging French military secrets to the Germans, but in fact his only crime was that he happened to be Jewish. The real culprits, generals in the French army, were conducting the trial on the grounds that if he was Jewish he was guilty of the charges.

Dreyfus was convicted, and only succeeded in proving his innocence many years later, with the help of the great French novelist Emile Zola.

Herzl was appalled by the trial and tried to understand "what it is that singles out the Jews in Europe for this different treatment." His conclusion was that the Jews were a stateless people and this statelessness was what set them apart from other Europeans.

In order to remedy this situation, thought Herzl, the Jews must have their own country, and the Jews of Europe must be mobilized for that purpose. The state would not be built clandestinely, but openly and officially. Herzl planned to go to Turkey to see the Sultan, who controlled the Holy Land, and obtain an official charter to create the Jewish state. The Sultan would gain a loyal, productive country and the Jews would have their own land.

Herzl called his ideology Zionism and worked feverishly to organize the Zionist movement. Though he did not obtain a charter from the Turkish Sultan, he managed to imbue thousands of Jews all over the world with his idea, and his followers flocked to him, impatient to launch the Zionist state. He admonished them to wait. He died at the young age of 44. Eight years after he began his work.

He had declared at the first Zionist Congress that in fifty years the state would be established, but in 1904 the prospects seemed much more distant. Upon Herzl's death, however, many Jews, especially young students from the universities and cities of Russia, packed their bags and set out for the Holy Land.

David Ben-Gurion, Yitzhak Ben-Tzvi, Levi Eshkol, Aharon Gordon, Berl Katznelson and others who would become prominent figures in the rebirth of the state were among the emigrants. They were young, idealistic, and attracted by the ideas of early socialism, cooperation, and other communal and national concepts.

They wanted to be workers, hired laborers, a proletariat. But work was scarce and the local Arabs were much better, faster, and especially cheaper workers than they were. Even the Jewish settlements of the First Aliyah preferred to hire Arabs.

The new immigrants of the Second Aliyah, as they were called, were determined to work, and if they could not obtain employment on other farms they would found their own farms and factories, but they would always maintain their status as workers. From this determination grew the concept of cooperative settlements, where common ownership prevailed and all had equal status.

This new type of settlement was called a kibbutz (commune). On the kibbutz everyone worked according to his ability and received a living according to his needs and the ability of the community to deliver it.

Not only ideology but necessity nurtured this concept. The only way to farm and settle the land was by a communal effort. A few years after the first kibbutz was founded another kind of cooperative settlement was established: the moshav. On the moshav every farmer had his own plot but marketing and purchasing was done by the community.

The Second Aliyah set the stage for the expansion of Jewish settlements and the building up of the land.

With the ousting of Turks and the entry of the British the situation changed. Though the British were in favor of the building of the modern Jewish state, opposing pressures were mounting.

The Arab population of the Holy Land initially approved of the settlement of the Jews. Palestine was a backward, neglected province of the Ottoman Empire and these new immigrants were bringing in innovations, development, and especially work and money. The advancement of the Jewish population brought with it the advancement of the Arab population. Arabs from all over the Middle East streamed into Palestine to find work and earn a better living.

The traditional Arab leaders of the area were concerned about these developments. A wealthier population was also one with more demands on the leadership. The change in distribution of wealth was already having an effect politically.

At the head of the Arab leadership was Haj Amin el Husseini, the High Mufti of Jerusalem. In the years to come his policies would lead the Arabs to defeat and exile.

He spread a rumor that the Jews wanted to usurp the Arabs' land and were buying up Palestine inch by inch. What he forgot to mention was that the Arab leaders were doing most of the selling and that they were reaping huge profits from the sale of mostly worthless property. Any voices of opposition to Husseini's allegations were silenced, usually by murder.

In 1920 Husseini incited anti-Jewish riots and many Jews were slaughtered in these rampages all around the country. The people most severely affected were the traditional, religious people who had been living for generations in the old cities. Husseini was afraid to touch the new settlers and immigrants. The riots recurred in 1929 and 1936.

An insurmountable barrier was beginning to form between Jews and Arabs. The British, trying to please the Mufti, curtailed Jewish settlement and immigration, but all they accomplished by these acts was to arouse Jewish indignation.

World War II saw enlistment by the Jews of Palestine in the British Army to fight Hitler and the Nazis. The Mufti spent the war years in Germany and Italy as a guest of their regimes. At the end of the war he returned to Palestine.

The survivors of the concentration camps of Europe were trying desperately to get to Palestine but the British, still attempting to satisfy the Mufti, shut the gates. The country erupted in chaos, with the Jewish underground organization fighting the Arabs and British, and bringing in immigrants illegally. The country filled up with Arab irregulars and British Army troops and turned into one big, fortified camp.

These pages: the domestic side of life on Degania Kibbutz, 'Mother of the Collective Villages,' founded in 1909.

In 1947 the British gave up, turning the whole question over to the United Nations, which decided to partition the country between Jews and Arabs. The Jews agreed, but the Arabs did not. Seven Arab states prepared to invade the country the moment the Jews would declare the State of Israel. They wanted no Jewish or Palestinian state to be created in this area.

On the 14th of May, 1948 Israel, declared its independence and for a year and a half the newly born nation fought off five Arab armies as well as troops and irregulars from the rest of the Arab world. There were 650,000 Jews in the area of Palestine and about 700,000 Arabs.

The Arab armies were hurled back one by one by the new Israel Defense Forces, and the State of Israel was established. Most of the Arab parts of Palestine were occupied by Jordan and Egypt and the Palestinian Arab state was not to be established. Many Arabs left their homes in the new Israeli state for the areas under Arab control, and many Jews from Arab lands were expelled and taken in by Israel as newly absorbed citizens of the State. Six thousand Israelis – 1% of the total Jewish population – had been killed in the War of Independence.

The young nation did not have time to lick its wounds, however. The situation on the borders was precarious, food was scarce, new immigrants were pouring in, and the land had to be developed. In the next few years the nation of 650,000 people would absorb nearly one million new immigrants: survivors of the Nazi concentration camps, Jewish refugees from the Arab world, and many others who had heard of the rebirth of the new state, exactly fifty years since Herzl's proclamation at the first Zionist Congress. They came from Yemen, Canada, India, Germany, and points between, all with the common purpose of being part of the Israeli people.

New towns and settlements were established, industries were developed, and an infrastructure was created.

In 1956 the Arabs again went to war against Israel. Egypt, the largest of the Arab nations, closed the Straits of Tiran, leading to Israel's southern port, to ships bound for Israel. Nasser, then president of Egypt, also nationalized the Suez Canal, which had belonged to the British and the French. The two countries retaliated by launching Operation Musketeer to regain the canal area and oust Nasser from power. The Israelis invaded the Sinai and destroyed the cannons which were manacing ships in the Straits of Tiran.

After the war's end, the Sinai Peninsula was returned to Egypt and UN troops were stationed between Israel and Egypt to keep the peace. The Arab states, who had signed only a ceasefire agreement with Israel, were still not prepared to sign a real peace treaty.

In 1967 the Arabs were ready to fight Israel yet again. Egypt, Syria, and Jordan, with an Iraqi contingent, planned a joint attack. The Egyptians expelled the UN forces and amassed troops on the border; the Syrians and Jordanians did likewise.

After a month of waiting in trenches for the expected Arab attack, the Israel Defense Forces launched a pre-emptive strike on the morning of June 4, 1967, in which they destroyed all the enemy air forces on the ground.

From the Golan Heights, the Syrians opened fire on the settlements in the valley below, as they had been doing periodically for the previous nineteen years. The Jordanians shelled Jerusalem.

In a series of surprise maneuvers, the Israelis routed the Egyptians from the Sinai Peninsula, drove the Syrians from the Golan Heights, and rolled the Jordanian and Iraqi armies all the way back to the east of the Jordan River.

In six days the Arab forces were defeated. The Israelis thought the Arabs would now be ready for negotiations. With all the territory it had captured, surely Israel would be considered a permanent entity with which the Arabs would have to come to terms.

The Arab response was not long in coming. The leadership convened in Rabat and proclaimed the three "no's": no negotiation, no recognition, and no peace.

Again Israel's desire for peace with its neighbors had been frustrated, and now it had to administer another one million Arabs, who had been brought up with a hatred for Israel and the Jews. As time went on and the stalemate continued, many Israelis began to call for settlement in the administered territories for defense purposes, and to bring a Jewish population back to what religious tradition viewed as part of the historic Land of Israel.

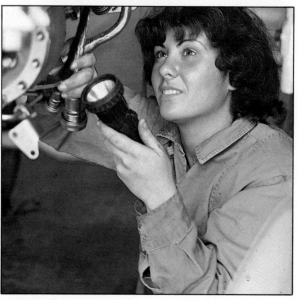

During compulsory military service young Israelis, both male and female, are trained in the use of a variety of weapons, including heavy artillery (above right, top right and facing page). Above left: Six Day War monument, south of Beersheva.

A controversy arose in Israel between those who supported settlement of the administered areas and those who felt the status quo should be maintained to facilitate their return in any future negotiations with the Arab states.

In 1973 the Arabs tried again. This time Syria and Egypt attacked Israel on the most solemn of all Jewish holy days, Yom Kippur, the Day of Atonement. Israel was completely taken by surprise, but again, after fierce fighting, managed to repel the Arabs.

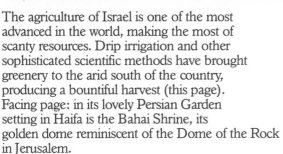

The agriculture of Israel is one of the most advanced in the world, making the most of scanty resources. Drip irrigation and other sophisticated scientific methods have brought greenery to the arid south of the country, producing a bountiful harvest (this page). Facing page: in its lovely Persian Garden setting in Haifa is the Bahai Shrine, its golden dome reminiscent of the Dome of the Rock in Jerusalem.

In 1977, Anwar Sadat, the president of Egypt, decided on a different tack: he would try to end the stalemate by peaceful means. In a daring move, the Egyptian leader came to Israel to talk peace with the Israelis, who eagerly awaited him. In the subsequent negotiations at Camp David in the United States, Israel yielded the Sinai Peninsula – a tract of land rich in oilfields and three times the size of Israel – to Egypt, and Egypt signed a peace treaty with Israel, the first Arab country ever to do so.

Sadat was assassinated for his initiative, but his peace treaty still holds.

The other Arab nations have not yet abandoned the war route and are still training their citizens to fight to destroy Israel. To add to the gloomy situation, until 1985 Israel was bogged down in a dismal war in Lebanon.

Above: at Kibbutz Yotvata sophisticated equipment is being used to restore some of the Negev Desert's ancient fertility. Right and above right: Haifa boasts much advanced technology. The water purification plant at the Technion scientific institute is powered by solar energy.

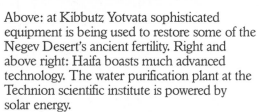

The constant strife with its neighbors is not the only aspect of the Israeli scene, however. Though Israelis are financing the war by paying the highest taxes in the world and are bedevilled with other complicated economic woes, the country has managed to create a thriving and vibrant society.

Israel is a leader in agricultural technology, designing innovations for desert agriculture, developing new breeds, and blazing new trails in agricultural engineering. Computer science is at an extremely high level, and Israeli companies produce the most sophisticated medical scanners in existence. Its color processing equipment is used by the world's major publishers and newspapers.

A magnet for tourists, Israel can boast not only monumental religious and historical landmarks, but attractive recreation areas and national parks, a flourishing cultural life, and an active sports scene.

The Israeli democracy is one of the liveliest in the world. Thirteen parties represent the nation's four million citizens in the Knesset, its 120-seat parliament, and every two Israelis have enough opinions for three parties.

Israel is now in its fourth decade, and one hundred years have passed since the beginning of the return to Zion by the First Aliyah. It is a fully functioning state, welcoming home its people from their dispersion all over the world – a 3,000-year-old nation reborn in its ancient homeland.